LOSING IT

LOSING IT

edited by

Keith Gray

ANDERSEN PRESS

First published in 2010 by
Andersen Press Limited
20 Vauxhall Bridge Road
London SW1V 2SA
www.andersenpress.co.uk

British Library Cataloguing in Publication Data available.

ISBN 978 1 84939 099 6

Printed and bound in Great Britain by CPI Bookmarque, Croydon CR0 4TD

CONTENTS

SCORING

Keith Gray

SCORING

It hurt. A lot. There was a lot of blood too.

I took my eye off the ball for only a second, maybe two. It smacked me in the face so hard that my feet lifted off the ground, my nose popped with a sound like bubble-wrap, and I went down on my arse in the wet mud.

The small group of spectators gasped. Everybody on the pitch froze. Then when they saw I wasn't dead, when they heard me swear, the rest of the team came rushing over. Matty was the first to get to me – it had been him who'd kicked the ball.

'Jase, I'm sorry, really sorry. You OK? I didn't... I wasn't...'

A couple of the others shouldered him out of the way, thumped him hard on the back, glared at him. I heard someone say, 'How're we supposed to win tomorrow if you go and kill Jase?' One of the spectators shouted, 'Nice kick, donkey-boy!' But it wasn't Matty's fault. I'd been the one looking off the pitch, not taking notice of what was happening on it.

At least a dozen hands were reaching down to help me up but I didn't think I could stand just yet. Mr Walsh pushed through to get a good look at how injured his star player was. He was a big bloke, whose 'big' might have been muscle when he was our age. He also taught German, but those lessons almost always included talk of *Fußball* because the school's footy team was what he really cared about. He shook his head at me, tutted. But couldn't hide a look of relief. I could read it on his face. Thank God it was my nose fountaining blood, not my feet. Even so, he didn't smile. He never smiled on the pitch.

'Hurt bad?' he asked.

I blinked twice. It was agony. But I just nodded.

'Good,' he said. He prodded at the end of my nose, making me yelp. 'It's not broken, you'll live.' He glanced over his shoulder at Tara standing on the touch line, hovering and concerned, but knowing full well Mr Walsh would never allow her to set foot on his pitch in this lifetime. When he looked back at me he was scowling. 'Let's hope it teaches you to stay focused on the game.'

He gave me a couple of tissues, told me to shove

one up each nostril to stop the blood. They just added to the agony, not that I was going to show it.

He gathered up the football. 'That's gonna have to do us, lads. Go get changed. But no one goes home until I've had a word with you all.' He waved over at the sports hall. 'Come on. Move.'

The team headed off. I got up, feeling a bit shaky and swallowing a thick gob of blood. One of the spectators cheered as I stood up, setting off a dribble of applause. Somebody else chanted, 'There's only one Jason Collins . . . ' We didn't often get people watching practice sessions but I supposed this was kind of an important one.

Tara had come to watch even though it was wet and cold. She was in big boots, hat and scarf, thick gloves, fighting against the wind under her dad's golf brolly. Beneath all those layers I knew she was beautiful. I wanted to let her know I was OK but didn't want her to see my face if my nose was splattered across it like roadkill. I half-waved at her, keeping my head down. Then held up eight fingers, trying to say I'd still be going round hers at that time, like we'd agreed.

She shouted, 'Are you OK?'

Mr Walsh put a heavy hand between my shoulder blades, steered me away towards the sports hall before I could reply. 'Save it for when you're off the pitch,' he growled into my ear.

A pale and panicky Matty kind of danced beside me. 'Honest, Jase, I didn't mean to. I wasn't aiming or nothing. I just—'

'Hell of a strike,' Mr Walsh told him. 'Just aim balls like that at the back of their net tomorrow, OK?'

Matty nodded, relieved I wasn't dead and he wasn't bollocked. I trudged alongside him across the school field to the sports hall, ignoring his fussing. I didn't know what I was more worried about: tomorrow's final, or my battered nose putting Tara off me. And it struck me just how much I'd changed these past couple of months because of her.

The changing room was loud, everyone's voices clanging off the bare walls. School uniforms were strewn across the benches, a couple of ties had fallen to the floor. As soon as I walked in I was asked how I felt, if I was all right, was I sure I'd be able to play tomorrow? I answered 'Yes' again and again. Matty, however, was on the receiving end of more stick and grief. And then the towel-whips started. I could have told everybody to leave him alone but in the mirror I looked like a horror story – blood and snot like war-paint, and bruising under my eyes. I was quick to get into the showers. I didn't dare rub at my nose, just let the water run over my face to wash the mess away.

A lot of lads hate the showers at the end of a games lesson; most think they're the worst kind of torture.

Getting bullied is always shit anyway, but getting bullied when you've got your cock out is a nightmare. At my old school we all kept our shorts on – would rather carry around a soaking games kit all day than show our classmates whether we had a length of pipe or a stub of pencil. When I'd moved here to Stonner Secondary last year I'd soon found out stripping off was the best way to avoid hassle. The rumour here is only paedos and virgins keep their shorts on. It's like, covering up just proves you've got something dodgy going on down there.

But what I couldn't figure out was, when had it all become a competition? Sex and stuff. Only a couple of years ago we'd been happy to avoid girls. Back then it wasn't that we didn't understand them, we genuinely didn't want to – most of them seemed so boring. We competed at football, or the Xbox, and they were the kind of things that had scores you could boast about. But then we hit fourteen, fifteen and getting a girlfriend became the biggest competition of all. And you had to do stuff with her too. Girls became yet another competition you tried to get a high score with.

None of the other lads in the showers were wearing shorts; even so, I'd have bet good money we were all still virgins. Apart from Tony Podmore – he always had eye-popping photos on his phone of this older girl he was seeing. But maybe after the match tomorrow I could join him, and be one hundred per cent truthful when I stripped off my shorts for the showers.

Eight o'clock at Tara's. Her parents were going to be away all night. So I was staying over. I'd nicked one of my brother's johnnies. She'd promised. And was it wrong that I felt more excited about hers tonight than the big match tomorrow?

We were all dressed and waiting for Mr Walsh. He wrinkled his nose at the heavy fug of Lynx when he walked in. He came over to the bench where I was sitting and leaned in close to inspect my nose. It had swollen to twice its size but looked a bit better without all the blood and snot. I'd tried to blow it when I'd been in the shower and it had felt like an explosion of red-hot razor blades in each nostril. Sniffing was much less painful. The bruising under my eyes was purple.

'Not as pretty as you were half an hour ago,' Mr Walsh told me. 'But that's not gonna stop you playing tomorrow, is it?'

'No, sir.'

There was a small cheer of approval from the team and a quiet rumble of feet on the tiled floor.

Mr Walsh slapped my shoulder. 'Good lad.' He stepped back, took up his usual position by the chalk board where he scribbled set-piece manoeuvres and match-play strategy. Feet apart, hands on hips, he faced us all.

'Big match tomorrow,' he said. And we chuckled – like we didn't know. 'Big, big match. I'm being honest with you, lads, it's the biggest I've ever been involved in. I've been coaching the football teams at this school for eleven years now, but you lot, you're the team that's taking me all the way to my first final. And I'll tell you here, now, I'm proud I'm sharing this match with you – with *this* team.'

We rumbled our feet in appreciation.

'You know I don't pick favourites, but it doesn't take a genius to realise one player in particular has a magic boot that's been out-kicking all the teams we've met so far.'

The chant 'There's only one Jason Collins...' started up. I reckoned my head inflated so much right then it might have popped my nose back into place, just like when you blow into a rubber glove and the fingers pop out.

Mr Walsh nodded, almost smiled, but not quite. He held up a hand for silence and immediately got it. 'I reckon his old team coach must have been crying into his beer when he heard Jason was moving schools. And right enough, Jason's the one who's been scoring all our goals. Twelve in ten games – I've never known anything like it. But he can only score those goals because he's got the rest of you behind him. He wouldn't have scored half of them without you lot feeding him the ball, backing him up whenever he ran. He needs you, all of you. Don't let him down and he won't let *you* down. That right, Jason?'

I clenched my teeth, nodded hard. 'That's right.'

Mr Walsh relaxed a bit, folded his arms. 'So there's not much more I can tell you, is there? You've got to do the business tomorrow. And you can do it, I know you can. Make sure you get a good night's sleep tonight.' He pointed to Moss at the back of the room. 'I know it's your birthday, lad, sixteen and that, all very exciting. But I want you to save the celebrations until tomorrow night, right? You're gonna be sixteen for a whole year but tomorrow's final is once in a lifetime. If I hear stories that you've been out until all hours fanny-arsing around, drinking and chasing girls; if I smell Carling on your breath in the morning; if you even dare to look a bit bleary-eyed, I'm not gonna let you put one single toe on that pitch tomorrow. You got that?'

Moss was quick to say he never would, never, not in a million years.

'It goes for all of you,' Mr Walsh said, waving his arms to take in the whole room. 'I'm talking to you like men, not boys. Make each other proud by showing a bit of professionalism. Stay in tonight. Do a jigsaw, play a board game. Then get yourselves to bed good and early.' He softened a little, almost smiled. 'Alone.'

There was laughter behind me.

'You know in the old days players were even banned from seeing their wives the night before a match? You lads heard that story? Footballers need a bit of aggression when they're on the pitch, when they're fighting for the ball. Storing it all up, keeping it all in, makes you aggressive.' He winked. 'Yes, lads, no sex tonight is what I'm talking about.'

There were grins and more laughter. From everyone but me.

'That includes with yourselves,' Mr Walsh went on. 'Give your wrists a night off, lads. I know that's gonna be tough for some of you, but if you want to be the first Stonner Secondary School team *ever* to win that final, you'll do anything, you'll give up anything, just to make it happen. For you, me, and the rest of the team.'

Someone at the back started clapping. I think it was Moss who shouted 'Three cheers for Mr Walsh!' I suddenly wasn't in the mood to *hip-hip-hooray*.

'The coach leaves seven on the dot,' the games teacher said, trying to stay gruff, but looking proud as hell of us all.

I turned away, just couldn't meet his eye.

***

Kirk thought it was hilarious. 'No way. Walshy really stood there and said, "No hand-shandies for you boys, I'm not having any pudding-pullers on my football team"?'

'Sort of. But that's not the point . . .'

Kirk rolled eyes. 'What a wanker.'

I hadn't known what to do. My big, swollen head had deflated pretty quick and I'd almost gone to Mr Walsh to tell him about me and Tara and that tonight was meant to be the night. *The* night. She'd promised. I'd tried convincing myself he'd understand. But deep down I'd known I was kidding myself. What did I want him to say? 'Give her one from me, lad'?

There was no way I wanted to talk to anyone else on the team. We all respected Mr Walsh, were always willing to jump the exact height he asked us to . . . Jesus, I felt shitty and all I'd done so far was think about disobeying him.

Kirk was my closest friend who wasn't on the team. He was taller than me, but skinnier. His chin was sometimes covered in the most volcanic spots you'd ever seen. We sat next to each other in most classes. He helped me cheat in maths. And French. Science sometimes too. He was weird in his own way yet I knew I could trust him to keep quiet. He also talked a lot about sex – so much that it was obvious he'd never had any.

'I can't believe you're even asking me,' he said. We were up in his bedroom. I had a Sheff Wednesday scarf pinned to the wall above my bed, ticket stubs from matches I'd been to see stuck here, there and everywhere, and two World Cup wall charts. I'd had a bedside lamp with a shade that looked like half a football since I was about eight and still hadn't bothered to get rid of it. Kirk had a life-sized poster of some model with massive tits on his wardrobe door. 'Wild nuns couldn't drag me away from a girl who'd promised me tonight was the night.'

'But what if it's true?' I said. 'What if me and Tara do it tonight and then I'm rubbish in tomorrow's match? What if I don't score? What if we lose the whole final because of me?'

Kirk shrugged. 'Can't see it happening. Footballers refusing to have sex? Come on, it's probably just a myth.'

'How do you mean?'

'You know, like you can't get a girl pregnant if you do it standing up. Or that fat girls come more.'

'Mr Walsh said boxers do it too. Refuse to have sex before a fight.'

Kirk nodded. 'Well yeah, I've heard about that loads of times. Everyone knows that's true.'

'So why not footballers?'

'Think about it,' Kirk said. 'A boxer's on his own, isn't he? And he's got to be angry enough to punch the living shit out of someone. But a footballer, what's he need to be angry for? Also, he's just one in a team. What's it matter if he had sex the night before and feels a bit slack? There's gonna be at least six or seven others in the team who didn't. They can get a couple of goals if they need to.'

'Not in our team,' I said. 'Did I tell you I'm the only one who's scored in the last eight games?'

'Only every time we talk.' He sighed, shrugged again. 'So don't have sex with Tara, if that'll make you feel better. But you'll feel like a right dick if you don't and then still lose tomorrow.'

'But tonight might be our only chance. Her mum's aunt's really ill or something, so her mum and dad have gone down south to see her. We've got the house to ourselves for the whole night.'

Kirk nodded. 'So *do* have sex with her, then. But you're gonna feel like a right dick if you let the team down and lose tomorrow.'

I scowled at him. He grinned back.

I checked the time. 'I'm supposed to be at her house in an hour.' I got to my feet and paced the room.

'Do you want me to go round for you?' Kirk was still grinning. 'I'll wear a Jason Collins mask, talk in a posh accent.'

'Great,' I said. 'Thanks.' I turned for the door. 'Thanks for all your help.'

He laughed at me. 'Look on the bright side. She

might not want to shag you after she sees that nose of yours. Problem solved.'

He had a small mirror next to his bed. I grabbed it and cringed at my reflection. I slumped down onto the floor, my back against the wall. 'When did it all get so complicated?' I asked.

'When did what get so complicated?'

'Stuff. Two years ago all I ever cared about was playing football, that was it, didn't give a toss about anything else. And everybody thought I was great because I could score goals. But it's not enough any more, is it? These days if you want to fit in you need to have a girlfriend too – and a good-looking one, not a minger. And she can't be frigid, she's got to let you shag her. Because you can't be popular and a virgin too. I mean, Jesus, who made up all these rules all of a sudden?'

'And when'd you go all philosophical?'

I didn't answer.

'But you're not a virgin, are you?' Kirk said. 'You told me you lost it to that girl from your old school. What was her name?'

He'd caught me off-guard. I tried to nod, tried to shrug. I couldn't remember what name I'd made up. 'Yeah. Yeah, her. But—' But my facc said it all.

'I knew it! You liar.' He crowed at me. 'You're still a virgin.'

I didn't like the way he shouted it. His mum was just downstairs. 'So are you.'

He spread his hands wide. 'Are we talking about me or you here? You're the one with the big dilemma, right? I was just eating my tea when you turned up all flustered and virginal, needing my advice.'

'Yeah, and how glad am I that I chose you to help me out...'

'Easy decision now, though, isn't it?' he told me. 'You've gotta lose your cherry, Jase. And I know half the school would want to lose it to Tara Madison... The male half.'

That was kind of the point. Tara was the whole point.

I couldn't pretend I'd been meaning to save my first time for anyone in particular. I'd tried it on with a couple of girls in the past but they'd always blown the full-time whistle long before I'd even got close to scoring. One had even given me the red card, which had been a bit of a surprise. But me and Tara had been together for two months now. She was fantastic, beautiful, funny, drop-dead sexy. I'd told her I loved her (and right at that moment actually totally absolutely genuinely meant it) so I couldn't get this idea out of my head that she was that particular someone I really had been waiting for.

'You got any nodders?' Kirk asked.

'Any what?'

'Dome-sacks. Cock-cagoules. Pocket-rocket-party-hats.'

'Oh, right. I nicked one off my brother.'

Kirk looked disgusted. 'One?' He rooted around in the chest of drawers beside his bed. Sellotaped underneath the middle drawer was a fresh pack of Durex. 'Best hiding place in the world. I know my mum searches my drawers but she never thinks of looking *underneath*.' He lobbed the small square packet at me. 'Pay me back next week when you get chance.'

'Why do you even have a packet of condoms?'

'Practice,' he told me. 'Got to be a quick-draw cowboy when the time comes. I'm like Clint Eastwood getting one of them on.'

I walked the long way round to Tara's. It had got colder but at least it wasn't raining any more. I'd texted my mum saying the bus had arrived but the guest house was a bit tacky. The match tomorrow was somewhere Nottingham way and I'd lied, saying we were staying overnight rather than having to do an early morning coach trip. I should maybe have felt worse lying to my mum than to Mr Walsh, but everything seemed so mixed-up right now, what did it matter?

It was dark and the lights were on in Tara's front room. And in her bedroom upstairs.

I walked round the block one more time.

We didn't have to have sex, did we? The stuff we got up to anyway, that was great. That made me feel like I was sinking into velvety earth. That made me feel like I had warm weights in my belly dragging me deep, deep down. Why did we need to do any more?

Because it would probably feel one hundred times as good.

As good as winning the final?

Loads of kids and teachers from school were going to be there to watch. Think of that thrill, that exhilaration, that fist-clenching, gut-busting roar whenever the ball exploded the back of the net.

Imagine if we won! Imagine the celebrations!

And we could win. Damn right. We knew we could. Mr Walsh and the team had worked so hard. *I'd* worked so hard. I had to score a goal in that final tomorrow. Had to. And what if what Mr Walsh said was true? Imagine if I screwed it up...

Yet being a virgin felt like some kind of anchor dragging around my neck. It felt like it was holding me back from growing up, from becoming an adult.

I wanted to stop lying about girls from my old school. I wanted to stand next to Tony Podmore in the showers and not feel intimidated. I wanted to say I love you to Tara in hundreds of different ways. Maybe I needed to leave being a kid on the football pitch. Maybe Tara was the future, and being with her was being an adult.

Maybe being an adult was all about maybes. I wasn't getting anywhere. I was cold.

At last I knocked at Tara's front door – then stepped back a bit from the light, hoping to keep my nose in shadow for as long as possible. And I thought maybe I should let her decide what was going to happen. If Tara meant as much to me as I said she did, surely she should be the one to make the decision? That seemed like a good idea. Yes. Tara's choice, I told myself. Whatever she says goes. And maybe then I'd have someone to blame if . . . ?

She opened the door, poked her head around the frame, all curly hair and big smiles. Beautiful. Stunning. She leaned out from behind the door and she was wearing a Stonner Secondary School football shirt.

That's it, I thought. That's a sign if ever there was one. Footy all the way. Concentrate on the big match.

'Suits you,' I said, grinning, reaching out to give her a hug.

She stepped out all the way from behind the door. She wasn't wearing anything on her lower half except for a pair of thin black panties. Her legs were so long and so smooth and so gorgeous.

I blinked twice. My grin went a bit lopsided, my arms held out there like an idiot. She was really being no help at all.

THE AGE OF CONSENT

Jenny Valentine

THE AGE OF CONSENT

Dora started it. My mum's seventy-three-year-old stepmother started talking about sex at the dinner table. Sex.

If that was me, or my big sister, Birdie, we'd have been shut down, told off, whacked round the back of the head. I'd have been sent to my room, without a doubt. I'd be throwing a tennis ball against my wall while everyone else downstairs got to eat banoffee pie.

But because it was Dora, nobody did anything. You can't send an old lady to her room in the middle of Sunday lunch. I reckon Dora knows that. She cheats at cards and steals all the nice biscuits and never cleans the bath for the same reason. My mum and dad don't seem capable of telling off somebody that old.

Dora chose her moment as well. She chose a good lunch, a special one, Birdie's sixteenth birthday. Birdie was going out that night, but this was like the daytime thing, the family celebration. The boring bit, Birdie called it.

There was us, of course: me and Mum and Dad and Birdie and Dora, that makes five. And then Birdie's best friend, Bell, who I can't quite ever stop looking at, and who always catches me looking. That's six. And Uncle Dave and Auntie Anne (seven, eight), Dad's brother and his wife. And their kids made ten, our cousins – Joe, who's eight going on forty-five and sometimes calls me 'boy' like he can't remember my name, like I work for him or something; and Chloe, who's six and has to live every day with a permanent column of white-green snot between her nose and mouth. I bet everything Chloe eats tastes like snot. It's enough to put you off your lunch, even if it is your favourite: roast chicken, roast potatoes, carrots, peas and gravy.

It was a toss up, I suppose, between the two of them, which one was going to put me off first: Chloe's snot column or Dora's sex talk.

She launched straight into it, like she was talking about the weather, or the curtains, or the football scores – like talking about sex was something everybody does at Sunday lunch. She started like she starts a lot of things, not necessarily at the beginning.

'Oh, he was lovely,' she said out of nowhere, like someone had asked, pouring gravy on her roast potatoes. 'All muscle. And *huge* down there.'

I'd never met Dora before she came to live with us. She was one of those relatives that you've heard about but you've never had proof they actually exist. She's not even related to us. Not strictly. She was married to my grandad, my mum's dad. He's been dead for ages. I never met him either. I wasn't born in time. So Dora was really nobody to me, when she came.

She just showed up one day in a taxi with a suitcase as old and wrinkly and flaky as her, and a nasty lamp that goes on and off when you clap (or when Birdie slams a door, so quite often), and a cat that dribbled. That's how it looked from where I was standing. All of a sudden Dora was there. Birdie says that's not really how it went, and I didn't hear Mum and Dad arguing about it night after night, like she did, before Dora arrived. I said that's because it's Birdie's bedroom next to theirs, not mine.

'Yeah, lucky me,' said Birdie.

According to Birdie, Mum and Dad invited Dora to stay in the end because they (meaning Mum) couldn't stand the thought of her living in a home. Mum says, 'Never put your loved ones in one of those places. *Never.*' She says, 'Shoot me before you put me in a home,' and sometimes Birdie says, 'OK, I will.'

I think if Dora hadn't come to us she'd have ended up somewhere Mum couldn't live with, so that was that. Dora showed up with her suitcase and her dribbling cat called Muriel. What kind of a name is that for a cat?

She moved into the spare room and she filled it with the smell of talc and perfume and old lady in about five minutes. She made piles of old plates and used cups that never quite made it back to the kitchen. She wore dresses and twinsets with bed socks and slippers, like her top half was somebody's secretary but her bottom half was going back to bed. She kept her bottom teeth in a mug. She wore glasses that made her eyes look big, like an owl's, and she read Mills and Boon books out loud to Muriel – to a *cat*. Plus she helped herself to everything, including whatever was in the fridge and the biscuit tin. Only Dora ever seemed to know where the biscuit tin was.

And now, to make things worse, she was talking about sex while I was trying to eat.

Chloe was breathing through her one clear nostril and Joe was showing off his perfect table manners and his talent for spelling. Mum and Dad and Dave and Anne were showering him with praise and banging on about something boring, conservatories I think, and organic paints. Birdie and Bell were whispering and I was looking at Bell, at the way her mouth moved and her cheeks went hollow when she whispered, and that's when Dora said it.

'*Huge*,' she said, and she pointed down there to make sure we all knew exactly what she was talking about, just in case we'd missed it.

Everyone went quiet. All I could hear was the gunk in Chloe's sinuses. The grown-ups stopped talking. Joe blinked slowly, like he was trying to catch up with what had just happened, like he wasn't sure how to function if the spotlight wasn't on him. I had a mouthful of food. I managed to hold on to it. Bell looked at something imaginary in her lap. I tried not to think about Bell's lap, how warm and soft it might be. Birdie stared at Dora, chewed up carrots on show.

'Don't eat with your mouth open, Birdie,' said Mum, like that was the crime being committed here. Birdie's eyes flicked up and her mouth snapped shut, and then she carried on staring. She blushed.

Birdie blushes at everything. She says it's a condition and she could get it fixed at the doctor's if she wanted to. I think she wants to but nobody's listening. I think it's one of those operations that either stops you blushing or paralyses you, depending. I'm guessing that's why nobody listens.

Birdie is called Birdie because that's all she used to say when she was little, apparently. She used to stare at the sky and point and say, 'birdie,' over and over again. I didn't talk when I was little, which is maybe why I don't have a nickname. I am thirteen and my name is Finn, which is enough. I don't talk much now, either. Bell is short for Isabella, which is a lovely name. Everything about Bell is lovely.

Birdie blushed and I managed to swallow my food and everyone else pretended Dora wasn't there. Joe started reciting his nine times table and Chloe just carried on breathing. Mum and Dad didn't say anything to Dora. They didn't even look at her. They went straight back to Dave and Anne and Fired Earth and Farrow and Ball like it hadn't just happened. I bet they thought if they ignored it, they could rescue lunch.

That would've been what they cared about.

Mum puts a lot of effort into lunch. Meals mean quite a lot to her generally. Birdie says the whole world could be collapsing around us and Mum wouldn't notice, as long as there were candles on the table, and fresh flowers, and parsley on everything. And as long as Mum's happy, Dad's happy – or not getting the cold shoulder anyway. Birdie says Mum lives her life like someone is watching and about to take pictures for a glossy magazine, like if there aren't pebbles in the bathroom, someone is going to judge her. She says Mum is obsessed with what other people think of her, what other people see.

I'm not so sure about other people and fresh flowers and pebbles and all that, but I like Mum's cooking. Her food tastes great. And the table did look nice, with these heart-shaped sort of sprinkles on it, and matching napkins, and the glasses that usually only come out at Christmas. Mum had made a lot of effort for Birdie; that's what it looked like to me.

And Dora was going to wreck it.

She said it again, a bit louder because nobody seemed to be listening, and she almost went cross-eyed with the memory of it. '*Huge.*'

I was looking at Bell and I couldn't stop. I didn't want to be looking at her while this was going on. I didn't want her to see me. I didn't even want her to remember I was there.

Uncle Dave and Auntie Anne hid their smiles behind pressed-together lips, but you could see it in their eyes, that they'd be laughing about it later. Mum wouldn't like that so much. I could hear her now, never living it down. I could feel her wishing Dora was Dad's relative to be ashamed of in public, not hers.

Dad said, 'That's nice,' like Dora had just told us she'd bought a hat or finished a jigsaw puzzle, the sort of thing you'd expect an old lady to say. Mum kicked him under the table but I suppose he had to say something. She'd have kicked him if he hadn't. Dad couldn't win.

Dora nodded, chewing on a mouthful. 'It was lovely.'

'Good,' Dad said, relieved, like that was that, like that was the last of it, and then Dora added, 'after the first couple of tries,' with a filthy giggle that shouldn't have been allowed anywhere near children.

Birdie groaned and put her head in her hands then, and I lost a couple of peas. I couldn't help it. They just popped out. I hoped Bell didn't notice. She wasn't the kind of girl that got impressed by spitting.

'Finn!' yelled Mum.

'What?' I said.

'That's disgusting.'

'I agree,' I told her. I couldn't stop looking at the picture Dora had made in my head. Just like that time when I was little and I saw the dead bird in the garden. I knew I shouldn't look. I knew I wouldn't be able to get it out of my head once I'd seen it. But I needed to know what the inside of a dead bird looked like, and what the maggots were doing, and if it still had eyes. It didn't.

'I think I might be sick,' I said, and everyone turned on me. Joe had that I'm-perfect smirk and Chloe was mouth breathing and I could see Bell thought I was a stupid little child. It was humiliating.

'Don't be an idiot,' Birdie said, and Mum said, 'Oh grow up, Finn,' and Dad said, 'That's great. That's all we need.'

Dora said, 'Sex is sex. You shouldn't be sick at the thought of it.'

'Thanks for that,' Mum said.

'I wasn't thinking about sex,' I said. 'I was thinking about a dead bird.'

'No surprise there,' Birdie said, and Dad said, 'Of course you were,' and Mum gave him one of her looks that means, 'See? He needs professional help.'

Uncle Dave and Auntie Anne just looked at each other, like they'd been saying the same thing for years.

'Dead birds?' Dora said. 'What do they teach you about sex at school?'

Everyone looked like they wanted to know the answer to that. I didn't know what to say. I didn't know where to start.

They showed us diagrams in Year 6 of the insides of our bodies. The girl parts looked like sheep's heads. The boys' looked like Gonzo from *The Muppets*. They showed us a video of a woman giving birth. I was worried about what kind of woman would let you do that, bring a camera. I had no idea there was so much blood and meat involved.

But it was way too late by then. School is not the place you learn about sex. Not when you can put Willy Wonka into Google and give yourself an education. Half my friends look up sex on the internet when their parents think they're asleep or tidying their rooms or doing their homework, the three main things parents want you to do.

I don't really get it, if I'm honest. My friend James showed me this clip on his phone once. It was all fuzzy and it looked like pistons to me, like an engine or a factory, and I couldn't bring myself to get excited about it. Not yet. It's all just pointing really, if you think about it.

So I didn't know how to answer the question.

'Mechanics,' I said. 'They teach you the mechanics.'

'Ooh, mechanics,' Dora said. 'I like those. I had a couple of mechanics when I worked at the factory.'

'Yes, Dora,' Mum said, emptying the rest of the bottle into her glass. 'We're beginning to get the picture.'

Birdie and Bell hid their smiles by drinking water, and Bell actually looked at me, without me looking first. I could feel her looking. The right side of my face went all warm with it. Uncle Dave and Auntie Anne and Joe and Chloe sat straight and waited patiently for something else to happen. Chloe rattled, like a straw through yoghurt.

'Dora,' Dad said, in this voice that was supposed to sound assertive, that I think meant he was trying to be in charge. '*Pas devant les enfants.*'

This means 'not in front of the children', the children who, Dad forgets, do French at school and are probably better at it than he is.

'What children?' Dora said, whose French wasn't too bad either. 'There aren't any children here.'

'No, Dora,' Mum said, and her voice was like this nasty, dripping thing that she let fall out of her mouth. 'There are five children here: Joe and Chloe and Bell and Birdie and Finn.'

'Sounds like a cage full of budgies,' Dora said, and she found herself very funny.

'I'm not a child,' Birdie said, and Bell nodded, which meant that she wasn't one either but because this wasn't her house she wouldn't be saying it out loud.

'Are you a virgin?' Dora said, and Birdie went the reddest, most livid shade of beetroot I'd ever seen. She blushed the hardest she'd ever blushed. Bell's perfect mouth opened into a perfect, stunned O. I couldn't take my eyes off it.

'Dora,' Mum said, pushing her chair back without meaning to, the way a horse kicks back against a fly.

'They just said they're not children,' Dora said.

'That's enough,' Mum said, but Dora clearly didn't hear her.

'Sixteen today,' she winked at Birdie. 'The age of consent. Will you consent, dear? If you get the chance?'

Birdie blushed, of course, and Dad gripped his knife and fork hard enough to make his knuckles pale.

'That'll do, Dora,' he said.

'She's old enough,' Dora said. 'It's legal. Who else?'

'Joe and Chloe,' Mum said, like a ventriloquist, her jaw clamped shut, hardly moving her mouth.

Dora looked at them both. I counted to six. 'Little Lord Fauntleroy and the snail trail?' she said. 'Too young. What they don't know goes straight over their heads.'

I couldn't help smiling at that. I couldn't stop myself.

Uncle Dave and Auntie Anne breathed in but I didn't hear them breathe out.

'Dora,' Mum said. 'I am warning you.'

'Warn away,' Dora said. 'I'm a grown woman. We're all family. And who's Finn?'

'Me,' I said, smiling. 'Hello.'

'Oh yes,' Dora said. 'Hello. Do you mind me talking about sex?'

She didn't just mouth the word, or try to hide it like most adults do when they're talking to kids and they see a word like that coming. She just said it, loud and clear. It rang in the dining room like a gong, hung in the air, ricocheted off Mum's favourite china.

Mum held her breath now too, like Dave and Anne. Bell counted her peas, her mouth almost moving with the numbers, her eyelashes casting shadows on the curve of her cheek. Birdie concentrated on moving down the scale from beetroot to strawberry. That's all she was thinking about. I could tell.

I had two choices. I could say yes, I minded, and go back to home decorating and the Guess-What-Else-Joe-Can-Do show. Or I could say, no, I didn't mind at all, and see where that took us.

I was going to say yes because I knew I was supposed to. I was going to say it because I knew that was what was expected of me, to save lunch and everything. I was about to.

But the thing is, I *didn't* mind.

Don't get me wrong. Listening to an old lady talk about sex is not exactly what I call appetising, and obviously I can think of things I'd much rather do with my time. But at least *something* different was happening. At least it wasn't just another Sunday lunch where nobody said anything even remotely interesting or memorable to one another, almost on purpose, almost as a point of honour. Like fresh flowers and pebbles. Like parsley.

I looked around the table at my own flesh and blood, like cardboard cut-outs all of them, like central casting. Sometimes I think we're all pretending to be a family but nobody actually knows each other. We could all be strangers just waiting for the same bus.

I looked at Dora. She grinned, and I saw for the first time that while she might look like an old lady, and smell and sing and eat like one, somewhere in there she was still a kid like me. A kid I could be friends with.

It occurred to me then how much Dora and I have in common. We're not allowed out on our own without being interrogated, both before we go and after we get back. We hardly have any money. We're not trusted in the kitchen. We have to do as we're told, just because. And nobody really wants to hear what we've got to say because it's not important enough and it's never the right time.

Maybe Dora was as bored as I was, keen to make this Sunday stand out from all the other, boring, well-behaved Sundays our family had ever had, ready to make Birdie's birthday lunch a hard one to forget.

I was happy to back her up on that one. Shoulder to shoulder, like the politicians say.

I looked at her and I grinned back and I didn't make eye contact with anybody else.

'No, I don't mind, Dora. You carry on. I don't mind at all.'

Birdie and Bell dipped their heads in unison, like two swans. They looked at me with something that I cheerfully pretended might be awe. Dad made a big deal of opening a new bottle of wine and making sure everyone's glass was full. Uncle Dave and Auntie Anne exchanged glances. Joe tried to get someone to test him on capital cities, but for once nobody was interested. Chloe wiped her nose on her sleeve. Mum drank her whole glass of wine down in one. Dad poured her another.

'I mind,' she said. 'This is Sunday lunch.'

'It's only sex,' Dora said. 'We all do it.'

'Well Finn doesn't, Dora,' Mum said. 'He's thirteen.'

I don't know why she had to single me out. I don't know why she had to draw attention to the fact, with Bell sitting there listening. Maybe I should've said I minded after all.

'I bet he'd like to,' Dora said. 'I bet he does it by himself.'

It was like being crushed by something heavy, the shame of it. Nobody knew where to look.

Birdie puffed her cheeks out and screwed her eyes shut and rocked, very slightly in her chair. Bell put her hands over her face, in pity or disgust, I couldn't tell which and I didn't care either, because pity and disgust are both as bad as each other.

'What?' said Joe, and Chloe said she needed the toilet. Auntie Anne didn't want to take her. I could tell she didn't want to miss whatever was going to happen next. Dave and Dad looked at each other and Dave winked. Auntie Anne got up anyway and took Chloe out of the room.

I wanted to disappear. I wanted to dic suddenly so they'd all stop feeling embarrassed for me.

'For God's sake,' Mum said.

'It's nothing to be ashamed of, Finn,' Dora said. 'You know that.'

Bell peeped out at the room from a gap between her fingers. When I looked at her the gap closed up again.

'You can't just sweep sex under the rug,' Dora was saying. 'You might as well fling it out there.'

'Well you've done that,' said Mum. 'You've flung it all over lunch.'

Dora popped in another forkful of meat and two veg.

'I was only talking,' she said, with her mouth full. 'I was reminiscing.' A fine mist of gravy sprayed her chin with each 's'. I waited for someone to mention it, but nobody did.

'Well I'm not sure I want you talking about my dad like that,' Mum said, 'about how big he was down there. It's not right.'

'Your dad?' Dora said. 'I'm not talking about him.'

'Good.'

She chuckled. 'Your dad was a bit average, seeing as you asked.'

I thought Bell was going to faint. I thought Dad was going to carry on pouring until the glasses overflowed and wine flooded the whole table. I thought of Mum's pink heart-shaped sprinkles all floating in it, like the lunch she'd planned had drowned.

Joe said, 'We're learning about averages at school.' You had to give him points for trying.

'I didn't ask,' Mum said, her eyes narrowed and

fixed on Dora, like she wanted to shoot her. 'But thanks for telling me.'

'I was talking about Danny,' Dora said.

'Who's Danny?' Birdie asked, and Dad said to Dave, 'Here we go, Danny with the big—'

'Don't you dare,' Mum said.

Dora said, 'Danny was the best man I ever had it off with.'

Anne and Chloe came back from the loo. 'What did I miss?' said Anne.

'The old lady's had it off with Danny,' Joe said. 'I'm a very good listener.'

Mum closed her eyes. She pinched the bridge of her nose like she does when she's getting a headache and I'm asking too many questions. She picked up her wine glass and sat back in her chair.

'To Danny,' she said, smiling at Dad in spite of herself, giving up because lunch was lost and she wasn't going to get it back. 'I'm sorry, Birdie, I'm sorry everyone.'

'Don't be,' Dave said. 'It's better than telly.'

'It's all right, Mum,' Birdie said. 'It's actually pretty funny.'

'A pretty girl,' Dora said to her, 'with all that adorable blushing. I bet the boys are crazy about you.'

She winked at Birdie when she said it. Birdie smiled and flamed up again. Bell pretended to see something fascinating reflected in her spoon.

'And we've all seen the way Finn looks at the other one,' Dora said.

'Bell,' Birdie said. 'Her name is Bell.'

'Yes. Well we can't miss the staring, can we, Bell?' Dora said, and all I could hear was the quiet and the scrape and ring of cutlery, and the hot, mortified pounding in my own ears.

'I don't mind,' Bell said. 'It's OK.'

(See? See what I mean about her? How nice was that?)

'I'm sure you're used to it,' Dora said. 'I should think you get it a lot.'

Bell smiled at her and nodded, and Dora put her knife and fork together and picked up her wine. She watched the rest of us while we ate. I could almost hear her planning what to say next. It was quiet for a bit. I don't think anybody dared speak.

Dad stood up and stacked plates and said something about a lunch like that making the washing-up look attractive.

'We haven't had pudding yet,' Dora said.

'I'll get it,' Mum said.

'I'll help you,' said Anne.

Joe and Chloe wanted to help too. They got all excited about it. Chloe's nose made a natural snot bubble, that's how worked up she was about helping.

Dave got up because everybody else did.

So then it was me and Bell and Birdie and Dora. I kept my mouth shut. I didn't say a thing.

Birdie and Bell were nudging each other and talking without talking. Then, 'You do it,' Bell said, under her breath.

Birdie looked at Bell and then at me. I pretended not to be there. I'm never usually allowed that close to a room with just females in. I tried to be invisible so I could stay. There was this change in the room now the others had left. Everything seemed altered, the light, the quality of sound. Both girls leaned in towards Dora. Bell's cheeks were a high pink, her eyes glistened.

'How old were you?' Birdie said, 'When you...?'

'When I what?' Dora said, leaning in for a different reason, leaning in so she could hear.

'Were you my age?' Birdie asked her. 'Were you the same as me and Bell?'

'When?'

'The first time,' Birdie said. 'When you lost it. When... you know.'

'When you weren't a virgin any more,' Bell said. Her teeth grazed against her bottom lip when she said the word, and I felt lucky to have seen it.

Dora shook her head. She folded her napkin and looked at her hands.

'Dora?' Birdie said.

Dora didn't look up. She shook her head again and said it wasn't such a good story.

'Oh please,' Birdie said. 'Come on, tell us.'

'I don't want to,' Dora said.

Birdie used this special voice she has for getting money out of Dad. It's the voice she thinks can get her what she's after. 'It's only sex, you said. You flung it all over lunch, remember. Please tell.'

'Have you got boyfriends?' Dora asked them.

They giggled and nodded and looked at each other. It was the first I'd heard of it. But then, why would I know? I didn't want to think of Bell with some good-looking bloke twice my size. I got this pain in my chest trying to picture it.

'Have you done it yet?' Dora said.

Birdie looked at the kitchen door. She waited a minute, to see if anyone was listening, to see if anyone was coming in. It was loud in there with the sounds of laughter and dishes. I could hear the shrill tones of Mum's voice and the shriller tones of Joe's.

'Not yet,' Bell said.

'*Nearly*,' Birdie smiled, 'Not quite.'

Then she and Bell looked at each other and smiled. 'Maybe later,' Birdie said.

'Maybe tonight,' Bell nodded. 'It is her sixteenth birthday after all.'

I wanted to say something. I wanted to make sure I'd heard them right but then they'd remember I was here and get rid of me. I was scared to breathe just in case that got me noticed.

'Maybe tonight,' Bell had said. I definitely heard it.

Dora didn't speak to either of them in particular. 'I was about your age,' she said. 'A little bit older. My father would have killed me, if he'd known.'

'Our dads would kill us too,' Bell said, and Birdie added, 'That's why we're not going to tell them.'

'No,' Dora said. I noticed she'd emptied her glass and poured herself another one. 'Girls got locked up for that sort of thing back then. Girls got beaten.'

'For what?' Birdie said.

'For not being virgins,' Dora told her.

'Really?' Birdie said. 'Locked up?'

'It wasn't like it is now,' Dora said. 'We hadn't got to bra-burning and the pill and all that carry on. It was different then.'

'What happened?' Birdie said. 'How old were you?'

Dora shook her head again.

'Please tell me,' said Birdie. 'I'd like to know.'

Dora took a deep breath in and sighed. 'I'll tell you if it makes you think,' she said. 'I'll tell you if you keep it to yourselves.'

Bell and Birdie nodded. I shrank down in my chair without actually moving. I just made myself very small and still and I think it worked because none of them looked at me. None of them told me to leave.

'You never forget the first time,' Dora said.

'Don't you?' Birdie said. 'Why not?'

'What was it like?' Bell said. 'Was it scary? Was it good?'

'It was terrifying,' Dora said, blinking into her glass. 'It was a shock. I can tell you.'

Nobody spoke. We all just watched her.

'Age of consent my arse,' she said. 'I didn't agree to it, I know that much.'

'What happened?' Birdie said.

'His name was Eddie,' Dora said. 'I was sixteen like you, but I didn't know as much. He was older. He took me out in his car. We were going for a picnic. I had no idea what he was after.'

'Seriously?' Birdie said.

'No idea at all. I was an innocent. I never thought it would be like that.'

'Like what?' Bell said.

Dora looked at her. She didn't pull her punches. 'Scared and half naked and wrestling on the rug.'

Neither of them said anything to that. There wasn't a lot to say.

'I'd never seen one before,' Dora said. 'That's the truth of it. I'd never clapped eyes on one and suddenly, there it was, attached to a man with designs on me. In the middle of nowhere.'

I felt a bit uncomfortable. I felt kind of responsible for having one in my trousers, even though I'd never used it on anyone. Even though I'd never had 'designs'.

'God, you poor thing,' Birdie said, her eyes wide, her hand over her heart. 'What did you do?'

'I liked Eddie,' Dora said in a faraway voice. 'He was a friend of my brother's. I had such a crush on him. He took me to the pictures once. He bought me an ice cream. He sat with me on the waltzer at the fairground.'

'Did you have waltzers?' I said. It popped out of my mouth before I could stop it. I blew my cover.

Everybody looked at me. 'I'm not a hundred and three,' Dora said. 'Of course we had waltzers.'

'Sorry,' I said, and Birdie glared at me like I was an idiot but she didn't throw me out. I don't know why. Maybe she just wanted to keep Dora talking and not interrupt her.

She said, 'So what did you do?'

Dora shrugged. 'I didn't like it. It hurt. I was frightened. And when he drove me home I didn't know what to say.'

'Didn't you say, no?' Bell asked. 'Didn't you say, stop?'

'No to what?' Dora said.

'No to Eddie,' Bell said.

'Well not so he heard,' Dora said. 'Not really. I tried.'

'What a bastard,' Bell said, and Birdie said, 'Bloody hell, Dora.'

'Did he know you didn't want to?' Birdie asked her.

'He didn't know much about anything,' Dora said, smiling to herself. 'Danny taught me that.'

Birdie asked her if she told anyone. 'When you got home,' she said. 'Didn't you tell?'

'Oh no, dear. I'd have got in trouble. I told you. My dad would've killed me.'

'But what about him?' Bell said. 'What about Eddie? Did you just let him get away with it?'

Dora shook her head. 'It wasn't like that,' she said. 'There wasn't anything I could do about it.'

Birdie looked at Bell and bit her lip. Bell's shoulders were high, like she'd shrugged and then forgotten to let them down.

'Whose idea is it?' Dora said.

'What?' Birdie asked her.

'Whose idea is it, your losing it tonight? Your giving it to some spotty Herbert you think is God's gift to women?'

'What do you mean?' Birdie said.

'Your idea or his?' Dora said.

Birdie fiddled with the hearts in front of her. She arranged them in a neat circle.

'His,' she said.

'Do you like him?'

She didn't look up. 'He's all right.'

'Not good enough,' Dora said.

'What?'

'He's not good enough,' she said.

'You've never met him,' Birdie told her. She was still fiddling with the little hearts. Bell looked anxious. I wanted to be big and handsome enough to go and put my arm round her and for it to mean something.

'I wish I'd lost mine to Danny,' Dora said. 'Think about that when the time comes. Is he an Eddie or a Danny?'

I thought about the question. I thought about all the men in the world being divided into those two groups without even knowing. It felt good to find out, before I needed to, which one I was supposed to be.

Birdie thought for a minute. 'He's neither,' she said.

'Then hold onto it,' Dora said. 'There's no rule that says you've got to do it now.'

'All my friends have,' Birdie said.

I looked at Bell. God, had she? Was her boyfriend an Eddie or a Danny? Did she know? I hoped she didn't. I wanted her to wait for some impossible point in the future when I was grown up and irresistible and I asked her.

'*I* haven't,' she said to Birdie, quietly, 'You know that.'

My smile wanted to fly off my face. I didn't care who saw it. I just smiled at her without stopping. I was still in with a chance.

Right then Mum and Dad and Dave and Anne and Joe and Chloe piled in, with birthday cake and candles and party poppers. We all sang. I looked at Bell the whole time and I sang and I smiled.

Birdie blew all her candles out.

'Make a wish,' Mum said.

'I did,' Birdie told her.

'What was it?' Joe asked.

'I'm not telling you,' she said. 'It won't come true if I do that.'

'Oh come on,' Dora said, 'that's a load of old wash and you know it.'

'What did you wish for?' Dave said. 'Driving lessons?'

'Make-up?' Anne said. 'A year's free hairdressing?'

Birdie stood up from the table. Bell did the same.

'I wished to always be able to tell my Dannys from my Eddies,' she said, and she looked at Dora while she was saying it.

'What?' Mum said, and Dad and Dave and Anne looked at each other. I wondered what Dad was, a Danny I hoped. I wondered about Dave. Everybody looked lost. It felt good to be the person at that table who knew exactly what she was talking about.

'Thanks for a lovely lunch,' Bell said.

'Is it finished?' said Dad.

Birdie smiled. 'We're going upstairs to get ready for later.'

And she squeezed Dora's gnarly old hand on the way out.

CHAT-UP LINES

Melvin Burgess

CHAT-UP LINES

It was Thursday night down at Rio's.

Thursday night at Rio's is a youth night. You'd never normally get someone like Samantha Harding down there with the rest of us, but she was a singer. She sang her own songs and played guitar, and you get a chance to play on stage at Rio's on Thursday nights.

She was on her own. She'd only just sacked Lee Sturmer for going with someone else. He must have been mad. I bet he regretted it later. Girls like Samantha don't normally go out with mere schoolboys, even schoolboys like Lee Sturmer. Girls like her don't bother with lads their own age. Normally, you'd have to have left school for at least three years before they'd even talk to you, let alone go out with you.

Samantha could have gone out with a rock star if there had been one living in West Gedding, which, needless to say, there wasn't.

'I'm going to ask her if she wants a drink,' I told my friend Drew.

'You're going to ask Sam Harding if she wants a drink?' asked Drew, and immediately fell about laughing.

'Seriously,' I said.

'Dream on.'

'What can she do?'

'Say no. Make you feel like a worthless piece of doggy-do?' suggested Drew.

'Thanks, Drew.'

'No problem.'

Sam had finished her set and was packing up her guitar. Just thinking about talking to her made me shake with fear and desire.

'Worth it,' I said. 'It'd be good practice anyhow. If you can chat up Sam Harding, you can chat up anyone.'

'Thought you didn't like chatting girls up?' said Drew. 'Thought you said it was a cheap trick, pretending to like someone just to try and cop off with them?'

'This is different.'

'How come?'

'Duh. Sam Harding,' I said. I mean, Drew's great, but she's a girl. Girls don't get girls.

'You won't dare,' said Drew. So I did. If Drew hadn't dared me I bet I wouldn't have, but I did. And you know what? Sam was really sweet about it.

'I'm leaving actually,' she said.

'So am I,' I told her. 'We could go somewhere else.'

She shrugged and said, 'Why not?' I looked around to see who else was there – someone I hadn't noticed who had just happened to ask her out for a drink at the same time.

'Really?' I squeaked.

'I said, yeah,' she said.

I picked my jaw up off the ground and tried to smile back. I just about managed to stay out of Lee's sight by hiding behind Sam as we left, and I gave the thumbs up to Drew at the same time. Drew rolled her eyes and shook her head, and I was the coolest man on earth.

We went to a bar round the corner. I smiled sadly at her when she said she'd have a beer. 'No ID,' I said, and waited for her to walk away.

'I'll get away with it, they know me here,' she said. And so a moment later we were drinking beer in a seat well away from the window where Lee, who wouldn't take kindly to seeing me having a drink with his only-just-ex, wouldn't see us.

'I don't know what I'm doing here with a boy,' she said. 'I've only just got rid of the last one.'

A boy. Wow. I was a boy in her eyes. Incredible.

She told me all about Lee, most of which I could have told her. Like, he's so busy thinking of himself that as far as he's concerned, empathy is some sort of building material. Like, he's so cool, he doesn't even know what hot is.

'So, the really cool kids are crap at sex, eh? That's worth knowing,' I said.

She laughed. I smiled. Then we sat. And sat. We sat a bit more. I sipped my beer and looked around. It was a bar. She sipped her beer and looked out of the window. It was a street.

That was it. I'd shot my bolt. I'd run out of things to say *already*. It was going to get embarrassing really quickly now, if past form was anything to go by.

I needed something to say, I had nothing to say, I needed something to say, I had nothing to say. I needed something... 'Er...' I said. 'Er...'

Sam looked at me expectantly. All I could think was – she likes songs, she sings. Words!

I didn't have any of my own, so I said someone else's. '*Young girls lie bedded soft or glide in their dreams, with rings and trousseaux, bridesmaided by glow-worms down the aisles of the organplaying wood.*'

Poetry! But I was desperate! I blushed even as I said it.

'Wow,' said Samantha. 'What's that?'

'Er, Dylan Thomas.'

She laughed. 'You know poetry?'

'Sure. You like poetry?'

'Yeah, I love it!'

I was amazed. I suppose it made sense, since she wrote songs, that Sam would like poetry. But Dylan Thomas? Sam's songs were pretty, folky things about relationships and the environment. 'Smart, bland and too much sugar,' claimed Drew, who had been known to write lyrics herself. She was just jealous because Sam could actually play and sing.

'It's *Under Milk Wood*,' I said. '*It is spring, moonless night in the small town, starless and bible-black, the cobblestreets silent and the hunched, courters'-and-rabbits' wood limping invisible down to the sloeblack, slow, black, crowblack, fishingboatbobbing sea.*'

'Wow.' She goggled at me. 'That's beautiful,' she said. 'That's so cool, that you know that stuff.'

'Cool,' I repeated. Samantha thought poetry was cool.

You know what? I know poetry. I learn it. I even write it – not that I ever said that to anyone except Drew, and even she's never got to read it. I never dreamed in a million years that it would actually help me chat a girl up; but suddenly, I was sitting here with Sam Harding looking at me with big, bright eyes, all because of my sad hobby. I opened my mouth and out it came. Loads of it, all the bits and rag-tags I'd somehow picked up. Shreds of Shakespeare, dabs of Dylan Thomas, reams of Roger McGough; love lost, love regained, Seamus Heaney, Edward Lear, Mike Garry, Simon Armitage – you name it.

I had no idea that I knew so much.

'How about this? Do you know this?' I said. '*I give you an onion. Its fierce kiss will stay on your lips, possessive and faithful as we are, for as long as we are.* Or this one? *Fools! For I also had my hour; One far fierce hour and sweet: There was a shout about my ears, And palms before my feet.*'

'Who wrote that?' she asked.

'I have no idea.'

And I'm sitting opposite Samantha Harding, and her eyes are bright and her lips are open and I'm just looking at her lips the whole time, looking at her lips. And all I wanted to do is lean across and kiss her lips and I was wondering, I was wondering... I was wondering if maybe she did as well.

'You really know your stuff, don't you?' she said. 'You must be the first boy I've ever met who knows poetry. That's amazing, it's so beautiful.' And then she asked, 'I guess you're doing English at A level. What books are you doing?'

And that's when I realised. She hadn't recognised me. I was so far beneath her, so distantly related to her species, she'd never even noted my existence. Why would she? The uniform was off, the street clothes were on. Here, I was like her – so she thought. At school, I was just one of several hundred other brats.

I was in Year 10. She was in Year – I dunno. Year 13, I guess.

'Oh,' I said. 'Oh, let's not talk about school. It's boring. School's not about anything I'm interested in.'

'Yeah,' she said. 'Yeah. I know. Me too.' And she shook her head sadly and looked into my eyes, and she smiled.

'You're a fast worker,' she said.

'I don't call this work,' I said.

'That's the best kind of work,' she said.

I was slinging out a line so long I couldn't even see the end of it, but when you're as far out of your depth as I was, all you can do is swim. I think that's going to be my motto from now on.

'Do you want to meet up?' I said. 'Saturday, maybe?'

'All right, I'll see you in here,' she said.

What it boils down to is this – she didn't know how old I was. Seventeen-year-old girls don't go out with fifteen-year-old lads. I never thought it would work, honest! I was just trying it on. I didn't think, I never thought for one second, that she'd actually say yes.

Drew was furious when I told her. 'She doesn't know how old you are? Well, you have to tell her, Brian!'

'I can't!'

'How do you think she's going to feel when she finds out? You're just having her on.'

'I'm not!'

'You are and you know it.'

We had a row about it in the end. I was like: look, I'm a decent sort of bloke. I don't take people for a ride, I don't diss them, I show respect. I hadn't told any lies, had I? It wasn't my fault if she didn't ask, was it?

Drew wasn't having any of it.

'Crap,' she said. 'Just because you haven't said anything, doesn't mean it isn't still a lie.'

I argued back. OK she was two years older than me. Three, even. But what of it? Girls go out with lads older than them all the time. So what's the difference? I bet girls lie all the time about their age. Some sort of sexism going on here, surely.

I did my best, but really, in my heart, I knew Drew was right. I had to tell her.

But I couldn't help wondering. How far could I get before she found out? Far enough for a snog? Far enough to cop a feel? Can you imagine that? Copping a feel of Samantha Harding's tits? That was like, I don't know, I can't even imagine it.

And what – I know this is ludicrous, but still, we're in La-La land here – what if I got so far as to get my hands down her pants?

Now, now – let's not get too far into the land of dizzy daydreams. But still, can you imagine that? Getting your hands into Sam Harding's pants? Only gods, movie stars and top football players could normally dream about such things. And yet, just imagine, maybe I, humble and lowly Brian Duns, could have such dreams myself.

But only if she never found out how old I was.

I went home that night and did my homework. Poetry. I stayed up for hours memorising the sexiest, juiciest lines I could think of: Dylan Thomas, Bob Dylan, John Cooper Clarke. Anything that might impress Sam Harding.

Even so, by the time Saturday evening came round, I'd made up my mind. I was going to tell her. I'm just too decent for my own good, that's my trouble. I planned it with Drew – how to do it without making either her or me look too much of a dick. I was going to break it to her gently. We'd go out, have a few drinks, I'd quote a bit more poetry at her. Then I'd own up and we'd both have a laugh and go our separate ways. And what sort of a dick is it has a chance like that and then throws it away for the sake of being politically correct?

It all happened quite quickly after that.

We had a great date. We went to this great little bar

she knew. No one even bothered asking me for my ID. I mean, if you're with someone like Sam Harding, you're obviously at least twenty three, so why bother? I'd borrowed a lump of cash from my sister, so I was well stocked. We talked about everything – poetry, books, songs, everything except school. She seemed to have rather taken to my idea that school was boring so let's not talk about it, for some reason. Afterwards, I walked her home and we kissed goodbye.

Yeah. You heard. We kissed goodbye.

It was on her doorstep to start with – just a bit of a hug and a kiss. She pressed up closer against me than she needed to. Then she slipped me a little bit of tongue and I slipped her a bit back and suddenly there it was, full frontal snogging. With a seventeen year old.

How cool am I?

'Mmm,' she said. 'That's too good to stop.' She grabbed my hand and pulled me round the side of the house so we could 'say good night properly'.

Yeah. You heard. She said, 'Say good night properly.'

And we did. Really properly. Big, big snog. It got really hot. I slid my hand onto her boob and she gave this lovely little muffled groan, but I wasn't too clear what that meant because she had her tongue down my throat. Then I slid my hand under her top and tried to wriggle under her bra but she pulled and twisted a bit and said, 'Not here, not here.'

Yeah. You heard. She said, 'Not here.' Translate that, if you like.

We snogged some more and then she let me, and then she let me...

Hey! Mind your own business.

Yeah, but, just if you were curious, you know that thing that normally only movie stars could dream about? Yeah, yeah. Right. That. You know?

What could I do? What would you have done? I was already in too deep. What could I say? Can you imagine it? 'Oh, no, sorry, Sam, I can't possibly feel your tits because you're older than me. No, please, do that zip back up. I'm too young to touch you there.' Really? I don't think so. And then, having done those things, to tell her then? That would be, like, bad manners, you know?

I know. I was being a bastard. I'm not usually a bastard, but sometimes it's just the only option. If the only other choice is to be Mr Nicey Nice-icles and miss out on the best night of your whole life – what would you do?

We had one final, lingering snog before she went indoors.

'See you tomorrow?' she whispered.

'Yeah, I guess,' I said.

'Come round here in the afternoon, about two,' she said. She turned to go, then she paused. Her mouth flickered in a half smile. 'My parents are out. We can hang out here,' she said. Then she turned and went indoors.

Tomorrow. Parents, not at home. Parents, tomorrow, not at home. And all I had to do was tell her my age and it would stop, just like that.

Drew was furious with me again, but this time it was because I wouldn't talk to her about it. Normally I tell her everything when I have a date – well, on the one occasion before that when I'd had a date. And she'd tell me the same if it was the other way round, except she never used to have dates back then. She just hung out with the lads – well, with me, really. But now I'd clammed up because, let's face it, if I'd told her what I'd been doing the night before, and that I was going round to Sam's house the next day for more, Drew'd have gone bonkers.

So I stayed in and didn't answer the phone all morning. And in the afternoon, I went round to Sam's place.

There was no question of us sleeping together, obviously. She's a nice girl, Sam, and it was only our second or third date. She just meant, you know, a bit of privacy. We had a drink, we sat down to watch some TV, we started snogging. It was enough, I can tell you. It was more than enough. Then we started, you know, a bit more. There was some pretty heated under-the-clothes action, I can tell you that much. In fact, certain aspects of the under-the-clothes action were actually fairly soon out-of-the-clothes action, which was already the most amazing thing I'd ever… well, seen.

It was more than enough.

'I can't do this,' she said suddenly.

'What?'

'I can't do this. It's driving me mad.'

'Sorry…'

'Come on.'

She stood up and grabbed my hand.

'What?'

'We're going upstairs. Do you mind?'

Language left me. I was speechless. She led me upstairs to her bedroom. She asked about condoms, but I hadn't come supplied. Why would I? I had never dreamed, not even in my wildest imaginings, that things would actually get this far. Apart from anything else, I was still a virgin.

That was something else I wasn't going to tell her right then.

'Boys!' she said. But she had some. So then we, then we, then we…

I was always scared that when it came down to it, it wouldn't work. That things just wouldn't stand up under pressure. But they did. Getting our clothes off was pretty embarrassing, but once we pressed up close to one another... you know. Naked. In bed. With Samantha Harding. You could have your dick chopped up and made into a sandwich for the bears, and it would still work.

It was the best day of my life by about ten thousand miles.

That was it – the big day. The day I lost my virginity and I owe it all to poetry. The power of words! Who would have thought mere word power could drop a pair of knickers at a distance of three years or more? I was the happiest man on earth – except, except that I knew I still had to tell her my age. Sooner or later someone was going to spill the beans, or she'd spot me at school in my uniform, and the penny would drop. Either way, it was going to be awful.

I'd pacified Drew by telling her that I'd already told Sam how old I was, and that we'd just had a laugh about it and decided to be friends. Another example of the power of words – lying. It was only a bit of a lie because to me it was just like, a truth that hadn't quite happened yet. But it was going to happen. I was definitely going to tell her, I really was, the very next time I saw her. And I would have, if she hadn't already found out.

She was waiting for me at the school gates. I knew. As soon as I saw her, I knew. She straightened up and stood there, arms folded as I got near.

'I'll just leave you to your girlfriend,' sniffed Drew. I think maybe she knew as well.

Drew left. Sam pounced.

'You didn't tell me you were in Year 10,' she said.

'Does it matter?' I squeaked. 'It's only three years? If we like one another?'

'You never even told me you went to this school,' she hissed. And her eyes turned red and filled up.

I thought of all sorts of things to say. Things like, 'You should have kept your eyes open,' or, 'You never asked.' That sort of clever, smartarse thing. But I didn't. I just hung my head in shame.

I didn't mean to hurt her, I honestly didn't. I know she'd never have gone with me if I'd said anything. I know that I am genuinely about a hundred miles beneath her. I know that her cred at school was now going to be so low, even the Year 7 kids would be leering at her. In one night she had completed the journey from cool, beautiful and talented to desperate cradle-snatching slut, and it was all my fault.

'If you ever, ever, ever tell anyone about yesterday afternoon, you are dead, you little shit,' she hissed. 'Understand?'

'I know. I'm sorry,' I muttered.

'Now fuck off and don't ever talk to me again,' she snarled. She stood there looking at me for a bit, and I could see her eyes filling up with tears again. I tried to tell myself they were tears of sorrow – it was all so sad! We loved each other but we could never be together. But I knew perfectly well what sort of tears they were really.

They were tears of humiliation.

Sam left. I waited a bit then went myself. Don't tell anyone she'd said. There was a problem with that. The problem was – I already had.

Not Drew of course. All my bloke mates. I hadn't meant to, it was going to be our secret, but I'd got on Messenger and Facebook and stuff when I'd got home and before I knew it, I was bragging. I'd told Alex and Tony and Ben and Henry, and who knows how many people they'd told by now?

I know. I'm a big mouth. But I needed the cred! Normally I'm the kid on the outside – the gimp, the nerdy one who knows poetry. Just for one day I had gone from zero to hero. Already, I was on my way down again.

By break Alex had already come up and said, 'Samantha Harding says you were lying.'

I looked sideways. I took a deep breath. I plunged the knife in. To myself.

'I was,' I said.

Alex looked at me with an expression of pure disgust. 'What did you do that for?' he exclaimed.

I shrugged. 'Dunno. I was bored,' I said, and smiled weakly. He walked off with a snort of total derision.

I spent the rest of the day being laughed at. It was pathetic, but it was all I could do. The girls were worse. The word, 'scorn' needs to be reinvented for when the girls are on your case. They made it clear, no way was I ever going to get to kiss a girl again, let alone shag one. It was touch and go if any of them were ever going to talk to me again. I was fifteen and all I had left were my memories. All one of them.

On the way home, I posted a note in her letterbox. I told her that I was sorry, that I'd already told some people but now I was going around telling them I'd lied. I was really, really sorry. But . . . she was still the nicest thing that had ever happened to me.

Yours, Brian.

I spoke to her for the last time a few days later. She came up to me at break. It was quite a windy day, I remember. It was unusual to see a sixth former out with us brats. She stood there with the wind blowing through her lovely brown hair.

Everyone stood still to watch.

'OK,' she said to me quietly. 'This is what's going to happen. I'm going to slap you round the face really hard. It'll hurt. I hope it does, anyway. Then I'm going to walk away, and in a few weeks or a few months, maybe – *maybe* – we'll be able to have a coffee and laugh about it. Maybe. As friends. Got it?'

'Got it,' I said.

'Close your eyes,' she said.

She really put some elbow into it. I could hear it coming. Crack! It left my ears ringing and my eyes watering. I stood there panting.

'There,' she said, nodding. And she walked off.

I thought – good move, as I watched her go. All the girls would think she'd done it to get her own back for me having taken advantage of her, and all the boys would think she was whacking me for lying about her. A win–win for Samantha. A lose–lose for Brian.

Things went downhill after that. My rating at school dropped even further and it's been bumping along the bottom ever since. I'm the kid who lied about sleeping with a girl. Why would I do that? Obviously because lying is as near as I'm ever going to get.

'Shagged any imaginary girls lately, Brian?' is the kind of exchange people like to have with me these days. No one has any doubts that it was all pure fantasy... except, I suspect, for some reason, Drew.

Sam and me never did have that cup of coffee, we never did get to be friends. She always ignored me when she saw me around, but once, just once, when no one was looking, she gave me a bit of a smile. And at the end of the year, when she left to go to uni, she sent me a note.

'Give me a ring in a few years.'

That was it.

Which was pretty nice of her. Of course, she's at uni, and I'm in the sixth form now, so it'll never happen. But the thought was nice. And, hey, you never know.

On the downside, Drew has never spoken to me since. Ever. Drew and me had been friends since way back. We were like 'that'. Then, overnight, whooomp. I was on the outside.

I tried to make up.

'OK, I was out of order,' I said. 'Are you going to hold it against me for ever?'

'It's not that,' she said. 'It's . . . ' And then she turned away and left me to it. I think she was crying.

She's changed a lot, Drew. She sort of, filled out, if you know what I mean. She dresses differently, too. Skirts and things. She goes out with a kid in a band now, James I think he's called. Somehow, before, I never noticed that she was actually gorgeous.

I reckon if I'd played my cards right, Drew and me could be an item right now. We could be going out together. I'd be getting sex on a regular basis. I'd have had sex several dozen times by now, instead of the once that I have actually had it.

I'd have a girlfriend. Imagine! I'd love to have a girlfriend.

Sometimes, down Rio's on a Thursday night, I look at her and her boyfriend and I just think – ouch. And sometimes she looks right back at me and she doesn't say anything, but I know what the words would be if she said them. 'It could have been you.'

I used to hang out with her all the time. Now, hanging out with Drew is something I just dream about.

But you know what? I'm sorry that Drew isn't my friend any more. And I'm sorry I hurt her, and I'm sorry I'm not going out with her. I guess she thinks I'm a sort of failed version of Lee Sturmer. I hate it that she thinks of me like that. I hate it that she's grown up and left me behind, when what was supposed to happen was, we were going to grow up together.

But.

You know what?

But wow.

It was still worth it.

DIFFERENT FOR BOYS

Patrick Ness

DIFFERENT FOR BOYS

The List

All right then, if we're starting out honest, here's pretty much everything I've done (it's not as bad as it sounds):

1. I've █████, of course. Everyone █████. They're lying if they say they don't, but █████ doesn't count, obviously. You can't lose your virginity to yourself.
2. And leading on from that, I've been █████ off by someone else, but who's been to a Year 10 party and not gone home without doing *that* in the coat pile? It's only someone's hands.

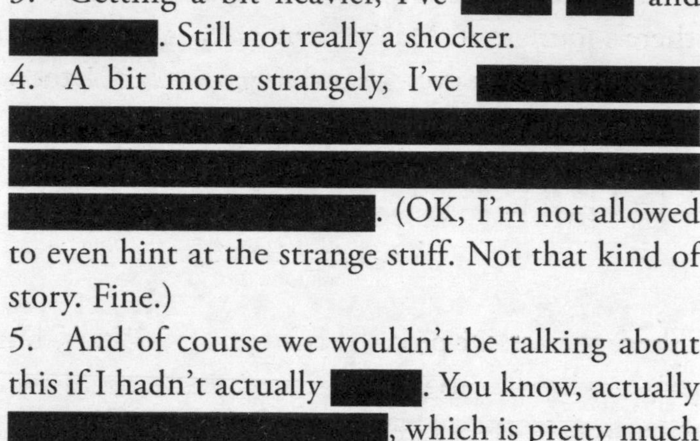

3. Getting a bit heavier, I've and . Still not really a shocker.
4. A bit more strangely, I've . (OK, I'm not allowed to even hint at the strange stuff. Not that kind of story. Fine.)
5. And of course we wouldn't be talking about this if I hadn't actually . You know, actually , which is pretty much the definition of losing your virginity if you're a boy.

And just so we're clear, it's not like I've done number 5 once or twice either. I'm not one of those chess-club virgins who goes into a closet and wonders if the real thing's happened. It has. Trust me. Although it doesn't really matter how many times you do it; you think it's going to make your life less lonely, but it never does.

I suppose my question, though, is where exactly on that list did I stop being a virgin?

Is it obviously number 5? Or can it happen sooner, like on 3? Or even 2?

Are there degrees of virginity? Is there a points system? A league table?

And who gets to say?

Because maybe it's not as clear as all that. Maybe there's more to it. Maybe there are people who'd *still* say I'm a virgin, even after doing numbers 1 to 5.

In fact, I might be one of those people.

Where It Starts

There are lots of places this story could start, but it might as well start on the first day of Year 11, when Charlie and me are sitting in geography waiting for Mr Bacon to get his seating plan in order.

'Well, this is taking █████ for ever,' Charlie says, then he blinks, surprised. 'What the ███ just happened? What are these █████ black boxes?'

I shrug. 'It's that kind of story. Certain words are necessary because this is real life, but you can't actually *show* 'em because we're too young to read about the stuff we actually do, yeah?'

Charlie nods solemnly at the truth of this. Then he smirks. '███████████████,' he says. His smile gets bigger. '███████████████████████████████████████.' He nods again. 'Cool.'

And just as he says, 'Cool,' that's when Freddie Smith walks in, which is where it all *really* starts.

'No █████ *way*,' Charlie says.

We watch Freddie check in with Mr Bacon, who finds his name on the list and points him over to me

e. Mr Bacon's great new idea for this year ing in 'quads' rather than just boring old ur desks pushed together in little islands around the room. Says it's meant to make learning 'collaborative,' but any fool could see he won't be able to control us like this.

The quads are alphabetical, so I – being Ant Stevenson – am sitting with Charlie Shepton, who I've sat next to alphabetically since primary school. And now here's Freddie Smith, who Charlie and I were also alphabetical friends with from way back, too, before he left after Year 4 to move to Southampton with his dad.

'Charlie Shepton and Ant Stevenson,' Freddie Smith says, coming over to us, grinning.

'Freddie ██████ Smith!' Charlie says, standing up and punching Freddie on the shoulder, even though Freddie's now twice his size. Freddie, in fact, is even bigger than me, not in any fat way, but like he just stepped off the Six Nations coach to buy a packet of cigarettes. 'Where the ████ have you been keeping yourself?' Charlie asks. 'It's been ██████ ages.'

'Mind your language, Charlie,' says Mr Bacon from the front. 'That's your first warning. Now, sit.'

'But it's blacked out, sir,' Charlie says. 'It's like I'm not swearing at all. ███. See?'

'*Sit*,' Mr Bacon says.

'Mum and Dad got back together,' Freddie

explains as we all sit down. 'After seven years, if you can believe it.' His eyes stray across the crowded classroom. 'Hey, don't tell me the fourth is going to be little Jack Taylor.'

'Aw, ███,' Charlie says, as we see Jack Taylor already being directed over to our quad by Mr Bacon.

'What?' Freddie says to me, confused. 'It'll be just like old times.'

Because the thing you need to know is that the four of us, me and Charlie and Freddie Smith and Jack Taylor, used to be inseparable. All through primary, anyway. Apart from always sitting next to each other because of our names, we lived in the same few streets, and for a while there, we were always together. Birthday parties and football teams and just plain old stupid hanging around.

Then Freddie left, and a few years later puberty hit and I suddenly got way bigger than everybody, like American football big, and Charlie got a foot taller without gaining any weight and Jack, well, Jack didn't grow all that much and though me and Charlie stayed friends, Jack kinda went his own way when we all went on to St Michael's Boys'. And while Charlie and me just did the usual – football, skiving off class, more football – Jack, well . . .

Jack got a little camp, if I'm honest.

He joined drama club. And choir. And wrote opera reviews for the school newspaper. And knew more than any drama-club-going boy ever really should know about Padraig Harrington (the golfer, don't ask).

I don't mean any of that in a bad way, though.

Because you don't really notice when it happens over time, do you? Jack's your friend. You like him because you've always liked him. And maybe one day you think, yeah, OK, he's gone a bit pink, but so what? He's Jack. And most of the time, you don't even notice.

Unless you're Charlie, and one day, you start noticing.

Since about last Christmas, Charlie's started noticing. And he isn't handling it well.

'Jack's a little █████ poof now,' he says, as we watch Jack come over. 'Hey, you can say *poof* without the box.'

Freddie raises his eyebrows. 'Jack turned out gay?'

'No,' I say. 'He went out with Georgina Harcourt all last year. He's just kinda camp.'

'He's █████ *gay*,' Charlie says. 'He was caught █████ to a bunch of sixth-formers last year.'

'No, he *wasn't*,' I say. 'Claudia Templeton from St Margaret's spread that story to stop people talking about how her boyfriend texted around all those pictures of her █████.'

'Oh, yeah,' Charlie laughs. 'That was *cool*.'

'It's never Freddie Smith,' Jack says, dropping his

bag on the fourth desk in our quad.

'Hey, Jack,' Freddie says. 'Heard you've gone all Graham Norton on us.'

Jack shoots a glare at Charlie. 'I see you've been talking to ████████ here.'

'Hey!' Charlie says. 'What was behind the box?'

'Hey, Jack,' I say, nodding a greeting.

'Hey, Ant,' he nods back, a little carefully.

'Graham Norton is a rich man, Jack,' Freddie says, still smiling. 'Nothing to be ashamed of.'

'Please,' Jack says. 'He's got a head like a watermelon. And have you ever heard him *sing*?' He gives Freddie a look up and down. 'And where've *you* been? Eating your way through Wales?'

'Aw, hell, don't even start,' Freddie says. 'I wasn't on school grounds five minutes this morning before the rugby coach grabbed me.' He nods my way. 'You've got pretty big yourself, Ant. You should try out for the team with me. Be nice to have an old friend around.'

'We play football,' Charlie says, before I can even answer.

'Quiet in the back,' Mr Bacon calls over to us, finally ready to start the new class.

'So, who's this guy?' Freddie says, lowering his voice.

I shrug. 'Just Mr Bacon.'

Freddie frowns. 'He looks familiar.'

'Nah,' Jack says. 'He just looks like if Gethin Jones was a mental patient.'

'God, Jack,' Freddie says. 'That's it exactly.'

Despite ourselves, we all see it. You could totally picture your sister going out with Mr Bacon, but then you could totally see him killing her, too. I'm about to say so, but then Charlie sneers, 'You want to *date* him, Jack? You want him to ■■■ you right there on his desk?'

Jack looks fake surprised. 'Are you *flirting* with me, Shepton?'

Freddie snorts under his breath. I laugh a little, too.

And then I see Charlie giving me a look that could poison a whole tank of fish.

CHARLIE

Charlie isn't a bad guy. He isn't, despite what's going to happen in the rest of this story. He's just got... *issues.* I mean, I know, yeah, fine, everybody's got issues, but Charlie's issues aren't too nice to him and they give him a rough time and that sometimes makes him act like a total ■■■.

But he's not a bad guy. He isn't. If the world were better, Charlie would be better. Try to remember that when the ■■■ starts hitting the fan, yeah?

Plus he's my friend. I've known him for a long, long time, and that counts for something.

'How cool is it that Freddie's back?' I say, sitting on my bed. We've come over to my house and gone up to my room, firing up my dad's old laptop that I got instead of the MacBook I asked for. We can hear it over there, failing to find the wireless signal floating around the house.

'Yeah,' Charlie says, nodding. He's sprawled on my floor, bouncing a football up and down. 'The *size* of him, though. Did you see?'

'Not much bigger than me,' I say.

'Bigger,' Charlie says. 'But you're fatter.'

'Screw you,' I say. 'I'm not fat.'

I'm not. Really, I'm not. I'm just big. I'm not fat.

'Jack Taylor's a mince, though, isn't he?' Charlie says, frowning.

'What do you mean?'

'The way he was practically *hanging* on Freddie. It was embarrassing.'

'Ah, Jack's all right,' I say. 'Leave him alone.'

'It shouldn't be allowed,' Charlie says. 'A poof like that. *Swishing* around school like Dale Winton.'

And we both smile, because we know what's coming.

'Bring on the Wall!' I shout suddenly.

'Bring on the Wall!' Charlie shouts back.

'Bring on the Wall!' I shout again.

And we do that for a while because we're young and we're stupid and we like laughing at stupid [illegible].

'That was classic,' Charlie says, still laughing.

'Better than that *dancer* they've got on now,' I say.

The laptop makes a sudden pinging sound and the screen goes black. 'Not *again*,' I moan, sitting up.

'Leave it,' Charlie says, resignation in his voice.

And then he's silent in a way where, somehow, I know what it means.

You ever noticed that about silence? That sometimes you can just tell what kind of silence it is? Sometimes silence is really loud, louder than anything.

Charlie's silence, for example, right now, right here, is asking me something, even though he hasn't said a thing.

And so I answer him.

'Yeah,' I say. 'OK.'

The List Again

You remember that list of all the things I've done? How long it was?

Everything on it, I've done with Charlie.

Last Boxing Day

It started last Boxing Day. Charlie called and asked if he could come over because his mum was getting even more drunk than usual. His dad's long gone, see, and his mum drinks. Nothing too special or interesting, but it doesn't mean it's not hard for Charlie just because it's common.

Anyway, my mum and dad know Charlie's mum, so they said yes pretty easily and he came over with every present he'd got, including an Xbox, because he was afraid his mum'd get into her torching frame of mind again, which she did once with all his school clothes in Year 9 (really, he had to borrow some of mine for *weeks*, made him look like a skeleton).

He ended up staying most of the week before New Year. Do you know how many times Charlie's mum called to check on him? Don't ask.

He slept on the floor of my room and we'd stay up all night talking and playing on the Xbox and going on the internet. You know, the usual stuff.

And then one night Charlie took us to a porn site. Nothing weird, just your run-of-the-mill naked girls. We'd done it before, plenty of times, but this time Charlie started talking. Talking about sex and girls and how long it'd had been since he'd

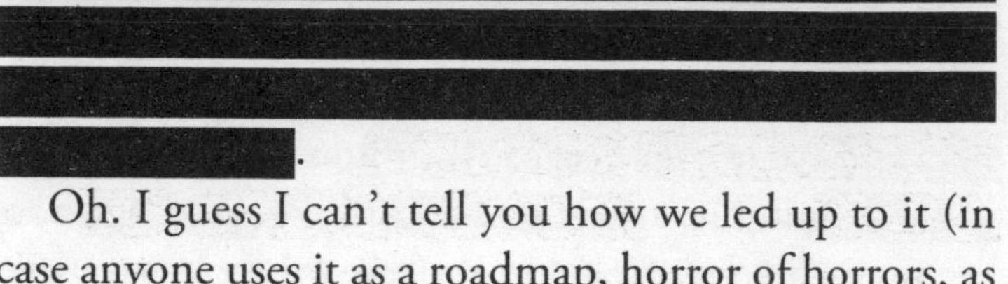
.

Oh. I guess I can't tell you how we led up to it (in case anyone uses it as a roadmap, horror of horrors, as if there aren't nine thousand and one examples of boys and *girls* our age getting together on every possible level; you can find that on CBeebies, for Christ's sake).

Whatever. Just to say that we were laughing about it all, like it was all a big joke.

And then there was this moment where it wasn't a joke, not even remotely, and it could have gone any way, in any direction, and let's just say, I was surprised at the one it took. Not necessarily because I didn't want to, but because it was *Charlie*.

Immediately after, it was like he didn't want to look me in the eye, though, and the next morning, he went right back to his house, taking all his stuff. We didn't talk at all until we were back in school and the first days were awkward and quiet and it took a while before things were back to normal.

Then it was half-term. Charlie asked if he could come over again. That time, it was easier to look each other in the eye. And that's how it's pretty much gone since then.

CHARLIE

Up in my room, Charlie's and he's and I'm and he's and I'm saying, 'Okayokayokayokayokayokayokay—' and so then he's and I and he's and I'm , and he until , too.

And then we're both breathing heavy and sweating from it all and he looks up at me and he gets this grin, this shy, embarrassed grin that says, 'Well, *that* was fun,' and says everything about how ridiculous it is for us both to be here like this, doing what we've just done. Every time, Charlie makes it clear we're just goofing around, that it's just a release until we both get girlfriends, and we spend most of our time trying to pretend we aren't taking it seriously at all.

Except for those few minutes when it's the most serious thing on earth.

'Football starts next week,' he says, after a bit.

'Yeah,' I say.

'We better make A team.'

'Yeah, right,' I say.

'No, I'm serious,' he says. 'I'm sick to

█████ death of C team. And we're both about a foot █████ taller than last year. That ought to count for something.'

'You might make striker,' I say. 'There's no way I'm making goalie over Olly Barton.'

He looks over at me. 'Have you seen yourself lately? You tower over Olly Barton now.'

'He's faster.'

'You're bigger. You'll beat him into the █████ pitch. Then we'll finally be on a proper good squad together.'

'If I'm so big,' I say, 'maybe I should join Freddie Smith on the rugby team this year.'

He looks surprised for a second, but then he sees I'm not serious. 'You'd get your fat █████ ass kicked,' he laughs. He looks up at my ceiling. 'Nah, you'll see,' he says. 'The two of us on A team together. Un-█████-stoppable.'

Then he turns to me with his shy, embarrassed grin again.

And that's the Charlie no one knows but me. The one who grins like that.

And I want to kiss that grin so bad I could cry.

But that's the one thing we don't do. Despite all that we've done, everything on that list, he won't kiss me. He refuses – so harshly I've only asked twice and not since Boxing Day.

We can't kiss.

Because that would make us gay.

Gay like Charlie sees all over Jack Taylor.

Padraig Harrington

'Seriously?' Freddie's saying. 'Padraig Harrington?'

'Three Grand Slam tournaments, he's won,' Jack says. 'Two Opens and the PGA Championship. He's an admirable guy.'

'So's Obama,' Freddie says, 'but you don't see me carrying around pictures of *him*.'

'I'm not *carrying around* a picture of him,' Jack says. 'It's for a project.'

'A project on golf? What class has you doing a project on *golf*?'

Jack sighs. 'It's for drama. We have to pretend to be a public figure.'

'And you picked *Padraig Harrington*?' Freddie says, but he's not laughing in a mean way.

'His accent's good practice!' Jack says, but he's smiling, too.

'Whose accent?' Charlie says, sitting down in the quad with us.

'This dude,' Freddie says, nabbing the magazine cut-out he'd spotted in Jack's papers and holding it up.

'That's just Jack's boyfriend,' Charlie says. 'He's got a thing for old men.'

'Padraig's not old,' Jack says, a bit too fast. 'He's thirty-eight.'

There's an awkward pause at how Jack knows this. And for how he called him *Padraig*, too.

'You're [illegible] sick,' Charlie says. 'He's old enough to be your dad.'

'My father is seventy-one,' Jack says.

Freddie looks surprised. 'Really?'

'Mum was his third wife,' Jack says. 'She "forgot" to wear her diaphragm one year. Now he's with wife number four. Which is weird, because wife number four looks like Lawrence Dallaglio.'

Freddie snaps his fingers like he's remembered something. 'Ant! I meant to say, I talked to the rugby coach about you, and he's all for you trying out.'

Charlie looks up sharply at this.

'I'm serious,' Freddie says. 'You could easily make B team, and maybe even a reserve for A.'

'Me and Ant play football,' Charlie cuts in. 'Always have.'

Freddie shrugs. 'Doesn't mean you always have to. Ant's grown into the right shape. Might be time for a change.'

Charlie looks at me. 'But we've always played football.'

'I wouldn't be any good at rugby,' I say to Freddie. 'I don't run very fast.'

'And that makes you good at football?' Freddie

asks. 'Come with me next week, give it a try. You might like it.'

'We've got *football* starting up,' Charlie says, as if Freddie's not understanding the point.

'You should join the Debating Society, Charlie,' Jack says. 'Your subtlety of thought is all they're missing to take them to the top.'

'Enough chatter, boys,' Mr Bacon says, suddenly appearing at our quad. 'Or I'll put you all on warning. You, too, Jack.'

'Aw, sir,' Jack says, all smiles. 'And besmirch my perfect record? You'd do that to a handsome boy like me?'

'Even a boy like you,' Mr Bacon says, smiling back despite himself.

We're all quiet as Jack watches Mr Bacon walk away for just a second too long.

'You little *sicko*,' Charlie says under his breath.

'What?' Jack says. 'I'm going to copy his walk for when I do Padraig Harrington.'

Freddie and I laugh, but Charlie just says, ' freak.'

Jack stares at him for a long, hard second, then he says, talking to me but looking at Charlie, 'I think you should definitely try out for rugby, Ant.'

WALKING HOME

'I swear to God,' Charlie says as we walk home that day, 'someone needs to kick that little █████ ass.'

'Jack's pretty tough, though,' I say, trying to make a joke of it. 'You sure you could take him?'

Which is the wrong thing to say, of course. 'Just because I'm not some █████ mutant giant like you and your new best friend Freddie Smith?' Charlie says.

'He's not my new best friend,' I say. 'Anyway, he's your friend, too.'

'He's probably a █████ poof just like Jack █████ Taylor. They're probably going off to ███ each other right now.'

'What?' I say, getting annoyed. 'You mean like *we* are?'

He stops right there on the pavement and glares at me. '████ you,' he says. 'I'm not a █████ poof.'

'Then why do you keep talking about Jack Taylor?' I say.

He keeps glaring at me, but then he says something I don't expect him to say. 'You trying out for rugby?'

I blink. 'What?' I say. 'No.'

'You trying out for *rugby*?' he asks again, even more angry.

I pause, a second too long, maybe because yeah, OK, I had thought it might be fun playing rugby for a change because Freddie asked his coach about me, about *me*, and Freddie—

Well, never mind about Freddie.

But I can see what Charlie's asking me.

'No way,' I say. 'You and me on A team this year. Un-█████-stoppable.'

'Too █████ right,' Charlie says.

And one more time, there's that grin. He looks like he regrets it, but he grins anyway.

The grin that makes my heart hurt a little bit.

More than a little.

Questions

And so do you see what I mean about the list? If Charlie and I are just doing all this as fill-in until the 'real thing' comes along, what does that mean? Does it mean what me and Charlie do isn't real, somehow? That we aren't really doing it to each other, but to some imaginary future girl? That no matter how much you go to football practice, it isn't really football until it's an actual game?

Have I even lost my virginity? Or am I just a virgin with a lot of practice? Because that's the way it sometimes feels.

And does wanting to kiss Charlie mean anything if he doesn't want to kiss me back?

One More Question

And by the way, is it poofs like roofs? Or pooves like hooves?

Who would know?

What Kind of Story This Is

One more thing before we get back to what happens. You know what Charlie said back there about Freddie and Jack? How they're both probably poofs? (Pooves? Seriously, is there someone I can ask?)

Well, OK, this is the kind of story where we can tell the truth, even if it is behind black boxes, so that's a good thing, but it does mean there's a whole bunch of things that this story definitely *isn't,* OK?

For example, this isn't one of those stories where one of us hunky young lads has lots of life-changing sex with Mr Bacon. First of all, *yuk*. Second of all, that only happens in stories written by horny middle-aged writers who think they look like Mr Bacon, all right? Doesn't happen in real life, and it's *so* not going to happen here. And third, seriously, *yuk*.

This also isn't going to be one of those stories where the great big tough rugby lad turns out to be a really self-confident homo who happily gets off with your humble narrator, much as that might be nice for certain humble narrators. I mean, yeah, the big rugby guys are gay just as often as everybody else, but I reckon most of them wait until university to figure it out. Then they all move to London and join gyms.

And finally, this isn't going to be one of those stories where everyone learns a lesson because the little camp fella turns out to be a total ladies' man. Jack did go out with Georgina Harcourt for all of last year, and I think they may have actually done the deed. I also know more than one girl who wants to go out with him, too, and they all say, 'Nuh uh, no way he's gay, he's just mature and sooo sensitive,' and then their eyes go all misty as they picture him as the perfect husband who'll listen to their problems and watch all the same DVDs.

And that's probably true, some of the time. But not here.

In real life, sometimes the big straight bloke is just a big straight bloke, and sometimes the kid that seems gay *is* gay.

Doesn't mean they're not still nice people.

Jack is gay.

I know, because over last summer, Jack told me.

And in return, I lied to him.

Sex Talk

'I'm telling you,' Charlie's saying. 'Five times. Five times in one hour.'

'Bull████,' Jack says. 'You can't even ████ five times in an hour.'

'Oh, Jack,' Freddie says next to him, shaking his head sadly. 'There's so many things wrong with that sentence, I don't even know where to begin.'

You know, the way teenage guys talk about sex, you'd think all of us were having it all the time, non-stop. OK, some of us probably *are*, but it's not nearly as many as brag about it. Maybe there's a boy who's enough of a moron to take a picture of his ████ and send it to his girlfriend and that picture gets passed around to *everyone*, and sure, there's the internet where sex is everywhere, but maybe people aren't actually having it any more than they used to. Maybe they just have better material to lie with.

For instance, Charlie's never had a girl, not as far as I know, not all the way, but he can talk about it like a porno director.

'Five times in an hour is nothing,' Charlie says. 'Not if the girl is a total hot ████.'

'Speaks the voice of experience,' Jack says. 'You've never had sex with anything besides your own hand, Shepton.'

'I think you're thinking of yourself there, Jack,' Freddie says, then he makes a ████ motion with his hand. '"Oh, Padraig. Come and get me with your big nine iron."'

Even Jack laughs at this, but then Charlie says, 'Jack's too busy ████ half the working men's club to need to ████.'

'The other half, of course,' Jack says, 'being otherwise occupied passing your bony ████ around.'

Charlie's face gets red. 'You little ████. You little ████ poof.'

'Oh, Jesus, Shepton,' Jack says, rolling his eyes. 'Why don't you just ask me out and be done with it?'

And me and Freddie are still laughing. But Charlie's not laughing at all.

He leans forward across the desks, getting his face up into Jack's. 'You're ████ gay,' Charlie says. 'Everyone ████ knows it. You can sit here and you can pretend to joke with the rest of us but you're a ████ poof and there's going to come a day when someone takes you down.'

But Jack doesn't back off. He just leans forward, too, and without taking his eyes off Charlie, blows him a kiss.

Which turns out to be a step too far.

Because suddenly Jack is falling back as Charlie lunges for him over the desks and Freddie's already on his feet, way faster than you'd think for such a big guy – no wonder the rugby coach wants him – and he's already between Charlie and Jack, holding Charlie back.

'I'm going to ████ stomp you into the ████ ground, you little ████!' Charlie's yelling, and Freddie's still holding him back and Mr Bacon's charging over and pulling them apart, too, and as Mr Bacon and Freddie start dragging Charlie to the door to send him to the Deputy Head, Jack looks up at me from where he's sitting on the floor.

'Oops,' he says.

Jack

It was one Saturday afternoon this past summer. I was supposed to go to the cinema with Charlie, but then his mum did something he wouldn't explain and suddenly I'm at the cinema by myself, yelling at Charlie over my mobile for not showing up and thinking I should just go home because what kind of loser sees a movie by himself? But then who shows up, but Jack.

By himself.

'Where's Georgina?' I asked him.

'We broke up,' he said. 'It's cool, though. We're friends.'

'Uh-huh,' I said.

And it was weird, you know, because like I said, I've known Jack since we were kids, since we used to call him *Jackie*, and though we'd grown apart as we got older, it was never like we'd had a falling out, and though he was already the campest kid in the whole school, it's not like I was ashamed of him or anything.

Well, maybe a little, maybe for reasons that are completely obvious.

But that little bit of embarrassment only made me feel bad. Plus, there was no one else around from St Michael's, so Jack and I went to the movie together, some incredibly stupid piece of █ about romantic vampires, five minutes into which Jack started making jokes and we pretty much laughed all the way through, getting shushed by the nine billion girls sitting around us.

And afterwards, of course, we were on the same bus back home and it seemed the natural thing to invite Jack in. Mum was delighted to see him; Jack was always the most polite of all my friends, and she made us sandwiches, which we took up to my room. I fired up the wheezing laptop and we started poking around the internet.

Which, apparently for me, is the cue for people to start Really Important Conversations.

'You know you can meet people over the web,' Jack said after we'd spent way too long looking up facts about Padraig Harrington. Did you know he's a qualified accountant? Of course you didn't. Why would you? Why would *anyone*?

'People like who?' I said.

Jack shrugged. 'People.' And was silent.

'You mean like on Facebook?'

He gave me a look to tell me to stop being such an idiot. 'Yeah,' he said, 'because Facebook is *so* cool. A bunch of housewives and forty-year-old trying to recapture their glory days.'

'Then what do you mean?' I said, laughing, because that's totally what Facebook is.

'I mean real people,' he said. 'You can *meet* real people.'

'And do what?'

He gave me another idiot look.

And then I realised.

'Jack, you're not talking about . . . ' I sat up. 'You're not getting groomed are you?'

He rolled his eyes. '*Groomed*. Please.'

'What are you talking about, then?'

And still he didn't say anything.

'Jesus, Jack,' I said. 'What kind of sleazy is going to meet up with a fifteen-year-old boy on the internet? You're asking to get yourself killed.'

'I haven't done anything,' he said, back-pedalling. 'I haven't actually *met* anyone. You know. Women.'

And it was that word, *women*, that made it all come clear, because it was such a false word just then, like he was suddenly trying to pretend we weren't talking about what we were obviously talking about.

'You're lying,' I said, my voice low. 'You've met up with people.' I reached out and grabbed his arm to make him look at me. 'You've met up with men, haven't you?'

He jerked his arm away from me.

But he didn't deny it.

'Jack,' I said. 'That's *so* dangerous, mate. I'm not trying to be a teacher here, but you could get your throat slit. You could get *raped*, Jack. Please don't tell me—'

'Just once,' he said, quiet enough to make me shut up. 'I've only met someone once.' He cleared his throat. 'It was horrible. Worse than you even think.'

'*Jack—*'

'And so I haven't done it again, all right?' he said, defensive now. 'I mean, do you have any idea how unbelievably *lonely* it gets? Feeling like you're the only one? It's not like I've got a lot of options for meeting people my own age in this little ██████ of a town, now do I?'

And then he looked at me. In a way that made me lean back.

And there was a silence that, once again, I knew was asking me something.

Asking me loud and clear.

This is just over the summer, remember? Not even two months ago. When I'd already been [illegible] Charlie regularly since Christmas.

And here was one of my oldest friends, someone who I didn't have a thing against in the world, someone who was fun to be around and who'd never been anything but a good person to me.

And of course I bloody knew how lonely it got.

(Jesus *Christ*, just that word, *lonely*, makes me feel so empty I don't even want to talk about it.)

I'd heard there were some gay girls over at St Margaret's who were dating each other right out in the open. But not at St Michael's. I mean, everybody knew somebody gay, duh, it's not 1980 or something, but not at *my* school. At my school, it was a secret, and you were on your own. I knew exactly how Jack felt. Of *course* I did.

Why do you think I was spending all that time with Charlie?

But I lied.

God damn me to my dying day, because the biggest sin you can commit is failing a friend. But that's what I did.

I failed him.

'Sorry,' I said. 'I'm not gay.'

Jack held onto my gaze. 'No? I thought maybe . . .'

I shook my head. 'No, mate. Sorry.'

He just nodded. 'I'm sorry, too,' he said.

I tried to lighten the mood. 'Can't you just look at internet porn like the rest of us?'

'Like the rest of you,' he said, all dry. 'Like the rest of you, sure.'

'Jack,' I said, reaching out to him. 'It's OK with me, all right? It totally is. I won't tell anyone, but it's OK with me.'

'Yeah,' Jack said, getting up. 'That's great, Ant, thanks.'

'Jack—'

'No, I gotta go.' He went to my bedroom door and then he went out of it.

And I didn't see him again all summer, not until classes started again, and we both had to pretend like nothing had happened.

The Final Weekend

'I'm not joking,' Charlie says on the Saturday after he lunged at Jack, 'I'm going to kill that little ████.'

'For God's sake,' I say, 'aren't you in enough trouble already?'

'I would have pounded him if that fat █ Freddie hadn't got in the way.'

'Charlie, we're kind of in the middle of something here.'

Charlie didn't get excluded for attacking Jack,

which is some kind of miracle, but he'd never been in trouble before, really, even with his loud mouth. Plus, Mr Bacon is soft, so all that really happened was that Charlie got hauled before the Deputy Head and given a bollocking (hey, look, you can say *bollocking*) and now Charlie has to write a letter of apology to Jack and to Mr Bacon for disrupting the class. Like writing letters is ever going to sort out anything, but there you go, it's better than exclusion.

'Are you playing football on Monday?' Charlie asks.

'Charlie, seriously, are we going to do this or—'

'I said, are you playing *football on Monday*?'

I lean back away from him. 'What do you think?'

He looks at me, and his eyes are like someone I barely even know, like someone *no one* can know. 'I think you're trying out for rugby.'

I nearly yell in frustration. 'When have I *ever* said that?'

'█████ this,' he says, reaching over to grab his shirt where he dropped it on the floor. 'I don't need this ███ right now. None of it.'

'Charlie—'

And I grab his shoulder to stop him, his bare shoulder, and for a second there, everything stops. He looks back at me, and I can feel his skin under my fingertips, I can feel his heartbeat coming down from his neck, I can feel the warmth of him just humming there, and he's looking back at me, all affronted and angry, but still the Charlie I know, still the Charlie I've known for all these years, and also the one I've known for the past ten months since Christmas, the one that only *I* know.

And I do a stupid thing.

I lean forward, my face heading towards Charlie's, and for a second, for a real second there, he doesn't move, he sees me coming and he doesn't move, his eyes full of fear but his head steady, and I'm going to kiss him, going to kiss him right on the mouth—

He shoves me, *hard*. 'Get off me!' he says, jumping out of bed and pulling his shirt over his head. He starts kicking our clothes around on the floor, finding his trousers and pulling them on.

'Charlie,' I say.

But he's already storming out, still buttoning up his flies, his shoes tucked under his arm, and I hope my mum doesn't see him as he goes or God knows what she'll be thinking.

Parents

A little while later, there's a knock on my door. 'Yeah?' I say.

'Everything all right, darling?' my mum says, leaning her head in.

'Yeah,' I say. 'Charlie just got in trouble at school, that's all. He'll calm down. He always does.'

Mum looks sad for a minute. She's known Charlie as long as I have. Known his mum even longer.

'You're a good boy, being such a friend to him,' she says.

She nods at me with a smile and closes the door.

Parents. I mean, seriously.

A Message

Later, I log in to one of the three networking sites I belong to.

There's a message from Freddie about rugby.

That's it. Just rugby.

But I feel a little feeling anyway. And then some other stuff that would really need a black box.

The Day The World Ends

Monday comes. That's the day it happens.

'Did you bring your kit?' Charlie says, thumping down in the seat next to me in our quad. He's hostile all over the place, but I know he's telling me he's going to forget about what happened on Saturday, that we can just move on and pretend nothing happened.

Like we always do.

'I brought my kit,' I say.

'*Football* kit?'

I sigh, because yeah, despite the message I sent back to Freddie (about rugby, that's all), this morning when I packed my bag, it wasn't with rugby kit. 'Yeah, football kit, but Charlie—'

'We'll make A team this year,' he says, almost making it sound like a threat. 'You just watch. Un-████-stoppable.'

'You won't make A team, Ant,' Freddie says, sitting down, Jack coming in behind him. 'You still have to learn the game, but I think you could be A team next year, no problem.'

Charlie just stares at him for a second, figuring out what he means. Then he stares at *me*.

'Yeah, Freddie, look,' I say, feeling Charlie's eyes on me. 'I changed my mind. I'm going to play football with Charlie again.'

'*Changed your mind?*' Charlie says. 'When had you ever made it up in the first place?'

'Charlie—'

'You said football. You *swore* it would be football.'

'Freddie asked me to think about it,' I say, 'so I thought about it. That's all.'

'We've always played football,' Charlie says.

'And we're going to play it this year. What are you so mad about?'

'You'd be perfect for rugby, Ant,' Jack says, [illegible]-stirring.

'Shut the [illegible] up!' Charlie says, too loud.

'Mr Shepton!' Mr Bacon calls from the front. 'You're already on your first warning. One more word and I'm sending you out.'

'You sure about this, Ant?' Freddie asks, lowering his voice.

I look at Charlie, still fuming. 'Yeah,' I say. 'I'm sure.'

Freddie frowns at me. 'Whatever, mate.'

My stomach hurts at the way he says it. And the hurt must be on my face, too, because Jack sees it.

And that's when it happens. A few little words is all it takes.

'Watch out, Charlie,' Jack says, smirking. 'You've got competition for the wife.'

And Charlie's eyes go wide, too wide, for a second too long, and though he's immediately pulling back and just being angry Charlie again, I see Jack look confused. And then surprised. *Really* surprised.

'*Jack*,' I say, warning in my voice before I can stop myself.

Because I'm sure, I'm *absolutely* sure Jack wouldn't be teasing this way if he thought it was true.

And I know this because I see him realise it the second I warn him like that.

'No way,' Jack says, under his breath.

'No way what?' Freddie says.

'Hey, ███ you!' Charlie practically shouts at Jack.

'That's it, Charlie!' Mr Bacon says, approaching our stupid little quad. 'Out!'

'Charlie . . . ' I say.

'No way *what*?' Freddie says again.

And I see Charlie's fists clenching and he's getting all red as he's staring at the wondering face of Jack, who's now looking over at me all astonished, and Freddie's looking at us like what the hell's going on? and the whole class is looking, too, and it suddenly feels like I'm naked there and everyone can see and everyone knows.

I see the confusion on Charlie's face, the *pain* on it, and Mr Bacon is approaching fast and Charlie's fists are up and here are all the people in the world he wants to hit, to take out all his Charlie pain on: Jack Taylor who he's made into his worst enemy, Freddie Smith who tried to make me play rugby and even Mr Bacon who's in the wrong place at the wrong time.

But it's not any of them that he hits.

It's me.

THE TRUTH

I hear him shouting over me. My hand's up to my eye and nose and I can already feel the bleeding. I've fallen off my chair to the floor, mostly out of surprise.

Charlie did hit me hard, but I'm already getting back to my feet when I realise what he's yelling.

'████ poof!' Charlie's screaming at me, spit flying from his lips. 'Faggot! Bender! Homo!' He turns to the class and even Mr Bacon, who's stopped for a second out of surprise. 'You know what this ████ pervert did? He tried to ████ *kiss* me!'

And I hear snorts of surprise from the class and I see the faces already starting to laugh.

Not Freddie or Jack, though, who are just staring at me.

'He tried to put his ████ hands all *over* me!' Charlie's still screaming. 'Ant Stevenson is a ████ faggot!'

'Enough!' Mr Bacon yells, finally getting moving.

'Deny it!' Charlie's screaming, pointing at my face. 'Go on, deny it!'

I'm standing up again, taller than even Mr Bacon and way bigger than Charlie, but I'm speechless. I'm just looking at Jack and Freddie, watching them see me not deny it, watching them realise it might be true, that it *is* true.

Why aren't I shouting back? Why can't I yell back all the things that Charlie and I have done together? That he's ████████████. That I've ████ ████████. That he's ██████████████ █. And that he's done all these things, willingly, *enthusiastically*.

With a word, I could bring him down, bring him down as bad as he's bringing me down now.

But I don't.

Because it's Charlie.

Even now, I can see how scared he is. How he believed all along that I wouldn't stay with him, that I'd pick Freddie over him the second Freddie walked in the door, that it's not even a sex thing with Charlie.

It's that he doesn't believe anyone would ever bother being his friend. That he's as lonely as I am.

And that it was only a matter of time before I abandoned him to it.

'Come with me *now*, Charlie,' Mr Bacon says, pulling him away and looking at me. 'Get to the nurse, Ant.'

Charlie's not yelling any more and he gives me a last angry look as Mr Bacon takes him out of class.

The other boys just stare at me, whispering between themselves. Laughing.

Jack and Freddie are still watching me. And I know they know it's true. Even if I did deny it now, it'd be too late, plus it makes sense once someone points it out, doesn't it?

'You ought to get to the nurse,' Freddie finally says. 'That's bleeding pretty bad.'

I wait for a second before I go.

Because somehow that feels like the last friendly thing anyone's ever going to say to me.

THE AFTERLIFE

The rest of the day is terrible. I won't lie. I go to the nurse, and by the time she's finished, it's all over.

Charlie got completely booted out of school. Not just for punching me in the face, but for 'homophobic bullying', too, a verdict that passes around the school even faster than what Charlie said and that pretty much seals my fate.

People snicker and stare at me as I walk by and there's like this force field around me on all sides that no one would dare to cross. I don't know why I don't lie about it, why I don't counter-argue, why I don't make Charlie the one in the force field.

Well, yes, I do, I guess.

I didn't think it was possible to feel lonelier. But there you go. Life will always surprise you with what it's capable of, eh?

There are only two more classes left in the day, neither one with Jack or Freddie; classes that I usually have with Charlie, so not only do I have everyone staring at me, there's an empty desk next to me to give them more room to do it.

I make it through. I don't know how. And as I leave the school grounds with the force field still in place and a group of boys singing 'Bender, bender,' just loud enough for me to hear it, I don't know how I'm going to make it through a whole school year of this.

And then.

And Then

'Hey, Ant,' I hear a voice call. 'Wait up!'

I turn to see Freddie jogging up after me. I stop, but I've never been so aware of eyes on me. On us.

'Hey,' he says. 'How's the face?'

'It doesn't hurt,' I lie.

Freddie just nods, then he looks at the ground. Again, I can feel all the eyes on us, and I can't believe Freddie's risking so much guilt by association.

He glances back up at me. 'I'm guessing there's some stuff here I don't know.'

I don't say anything, just look away.

'But I'm thinking this probably means you can try out for rugby now?' he says.

I look up. 'What?'

Freddie shrugs. 'If you can take a hit like that and get right back up, that's pretty much all rugby is. You're made for it.'

'Freddie—'

'You're going to get █,' he interrupts, looking around at the staring eyes on us, holding them until they look away. 'Everyone's going to give you █ for a while.' He shrugs again. 'So what you've got to do is make sure they know you don't care. Show them you don't. Try out for rugby. It'll pass.'

'You don't . . .' I swallow, still tasting the blood at the back of my throat. 'You don't care?'

He grins. 'As long as you don't try to kiss *me*.'

I stare at him, unbelieving.

'Look, I'm late for practice,' he says. 'But the next one's on Wednesday.' He hits me hard on the shoulder. 'I expect to see you there, bruiser.'

THE EVENING AFTER THE END OF THE WORLD

The bell goes at my front door about six that night. I hear it from my room, where I'm busy spending my time avoiding writing Mr Bacon's geography homework. A minute later, there's a knock on my bedroom door. I think it's my mum, so I just say, 'What?'

But it's Jack who pokes his head in.

I don't say anything when I see him, so he just steps into the room and shuts the door. We stare at each other for a second.

'Your mum thinks you did that playing rugby,' he finally says, nodding at my black eye.

'Parents say they want to know the truth,' I say, 'but they never really mean it.'

'Tell me about it,' he says, crossing his arms, looking at the floor, the walls, anything but my face.

'If you came here for an apology,' I say. 'I'm sorry.'

He glances at me. 'Apology for what?'

'Over the summer,' I say. 'You tried to tell me and I—'

'Oh, please,' he says. 'Like I didn't know you were lying.'

I blink. 'You knew?'

'It was obvious,' he says. 'Well, obvious to *me*, but that's probably only because I was looking.' He makes a surprised face. 'Didn't know about you and Charlie, though. That was a shocker.' He laughs, once, then looks more serious. 'If I'd known, I wouldn't have teased you.'

'I know,' I say.

He's quiet for a minute and then finally comes away from the door, flopping down on the edge of my bed, next to me but not too close. 'It isn't easy,' he says, 'having people think that about you. But most of them don't care, not *really*. They just love having something new to beat you up with. You have to show them it won't work, and then they'll go back to killing Ginger Mike.'

I breathe out, long and tired. 'That's what Freddie said.'

'Ah, big lovely Freddie.' Jack looks over at me. 'Straight, you know. As a Roman road. No matter how much you might wish him otherwise.'

'I know,' I say. 'I have to say, as stupid as it sounds, I don't think Charlie's gay either. I think he just needed someone. Someone who cared only for him.'

Jack sighs. 'You always *were* soft-hearted, Ant.'

'Thanks.'

'No, I meant soft-*headed*.'

'That, too.'

And for a minute, it feels like I'm going to cry, it really does, about how empty it all feels, about how difficult things are going to be at school for a while, about how much relief there is in still having friends like Freddie and Jack.

About how mad I am at Charlie.

About how bad it feels, too, that I've lost him.

I don't think Jack knows what to do with me looking so upset, so he starts awkwardly slapping me on the back, like he's trying to comfort me but is a little afraid to.

'It'll be all right,' he says. 'It will, you know. School will be fine, and even if it isn't, school isn't the rest of your life. Not even close.'

'I know,' I say, my voice a little rough.

We just sit there like that for a long, long time, letting night fall outside, not saying anything at all, just the two of us sitting there, waiting for the month or year or whenever in our lives when we're allowed to stop being lonely.

'Jack,' I say, when it's almost too dark to see. 'Can I ask you something? Something I've always wanted to know?'

'OK,' he says, a little suspiciously.

I turn to him. 'Padraig *Harrington*?'

Jack seems surprised into an honest answer. 'He looks like he'd never hurt you.'

I don't know what to say to this, so I don't say anything, just lower my eyes.

'Plus,' Jack says, 'he walks like he's making milkshakes in his pockets.'

I snort with laughter.

'What?' Jack says, all innocent-sounding. 'I like *cooking*.'

I laugh again. And then I look at him to find he's looking back at me.

'Can I make a guess about something?' he says.

'What?' I ask.

And he leans forward, just a little, then a little more.

And I don't move towards him. But I don't move back either.

And he reaches me.

And he kisses me.

Gently so as not to bump my nose or eye, he presses his lips to mine.

And for a second, for a minute, for *ever*, every nerve in my body is right there, right at the point where we're touching.

And *boom*, I think.

That's it.

DIFFERENT FOR BOYS

I think it's different for boys, boys like me anyway. I think I get to choose when I stop calling myself a virgin. I don't think there are any rules or any specific moment where anyone can say, yep, that's it, that's where you're not a virgin any more.

I think *I'm* the one who says.

Because nothing I did with Charlie ever *once* felt like that kiss with Jack.

And yeah, it'd be romantic and swooning and a perfect ending for the story if that kiss was all we ended up doing.

But please, we're teenage boys with teenage hormones and no chance of anyone getting pregnant.

What do you *think* we did next?

I'll tell you. We ██████████ and then we ██████████ and that was just unbelievably great so ██████████ and then ██████████ and then we ██████████

.

And then, after a while, it all sort of morphed into us just talking, which we did for a bit, and then a bit more than that, and then Jack went on home.

Now don't get me wrong here. I'm not saying this is the moment where I found the love of my life. Jack's a really nice guy and a good friend, but I'm not really his type – I look *nothing* like Padraig Harrington – and he's probably not really mine, come to think of it. Besides, there's a whole life out there left for both of us.

At least, now it feels like there might be.

And I won't say for definite if it was the kiss that felt like the moment when I lost my virginity, number 6 added to the list, because now that I think about it, that really *is* the kind of private thing that should go behind a black box and not all of this swearing and sex crap. You can only lose it once, and maybe, finally, it's just private.

, you know?

But I will say this.

Through that whole night, all of it, I didn't sleep a wink. I was worried about the next day at school, sure I was, but I also kept putting my hand up to my lips, pressing them lightly, feeling where Jack's lips touched mine, actually *touched* them.

Just to keep reminding myself that it actually happened.

CHARLOTTE

Mary Hooper

CHARLOTTE

When Charlotte's mother died there was no money to bury her, so her body was left where she finally breathed her last, in a corner of the small room where they lived in St Giles Lane. There she lay for three days, covered with a ragged blue curtain, until the neighbours had collected enough money from the others in the house to have the body taken to a paupers' burial ground. No one went to the funeral, no friends or neighbours – and certainly not Charlotte or her little brothers – for no one had the black clothes, the fare to the cemetery, or could spare a working day. Besides, it was hardly worth it, for a pauper's interment did not include any ceremonials or even a drink to speed the dead person on their last journey, but just two drunken gravediggers opening up a well-used trench in the ground, and a few mumbled words from a parson.

Charlotte was fifteen and George and Albert were seven and eight respectively. Two other children – a boy and a girl – had been born in the years between Charlotte's birth and those of the boys, but neither had survived beyond the age of two. In the days following her mother's death, Charlotte often thought about the dead children, wondering how she would have managed if there had been five mouths to feed instead of three. But then, she thought on other occasions, what if the two missing children had had some special talent: amazing tumbling skills to draw the ha'pennies of those waiting outside the theatres, for instance, or fingers that were deft and skilled at lace-making or could sew on buttons as fast as a flea could run across a bedsheet. If that had been the case, the one talented child might have earned enough to keep them all.

But no, for better or worse it was just the three of them, and Charlotte intended to earn money the way her mother had done before her, by sewing shirts at home. She envisaged no problems with this, for she'd been helping to oversew buttonholes since she was a child of six and had become quick and deft at it.

For a week after their mother died, however, Charlotte did not – could not – sew buttonholes or anything else, but simply lay on the mattress she'd shared with her ma and wept. The boys cried pitifully too, and between times slept, and occasionally woke up to eat whatever their neighbours had left on the landing outside their room: hot potatoes, boiled puddings, an onion pasty and, once, a small meat pie. The neighbours, poor as mice, had hungry children of their own, so could only manage to give away a little food, but luckily for George and Albert (who were always hungry, despite their grief), Charlotte had lost her appetite and invariably gave them her portion.

A week or so went by and then one day George and Albert looked outside the door mid-morning as usual, to see what had been left for them.

'There's nothing!' Albert said, surveying the bare floorboards up and down the corridor. 'Someone's taken our food!'

'But I'm *hungry*!' said George, putting his hand in his mouth and sucking his fingers.

Charlotte rose from the mattress, checked outside the door and tiptoed along the passageway to the top of the stairs. Albert was right. No food had been left for them. As she began to walk back, a door in the passageway opened and she turned to see the young woman who lived in the next room, Mrs Kyle, standing there smiling at her sympathetically. 'It's not because people don't care,' said Mrs Kyle, 'but because they think you ought to begin to fend for yourself now. The longer you leave it, you know, the harder it'll be.'

Charlotte nodded and, before she went back, thanked the woman for all she'd done. Mrs Kyle, she knew, could ill afford to spare any food. Not much older than Charlotte, she already had two infant children and a husband who spent most of his wages at the Dog and Duck.

The rest of that day Charlotte and her brothers had nothing to eat except a hunk of bread, but the following day Charlotte was up early to organise them and get them out to work. Before their mother's death, George had gone out collecting cigar butts in the streets to sell to a second-smoke cigar maker, and Albert had made a tidy amount working for a dog-duffer: a man who received stolen pedigree dogs, changed their appearance by dyeing their fur, and then sold them on to unsuspecting new owners. Charlotte hoped that they'd be able to continue with these occupations and that life would go on as before until her sweetheart, Joe, came for her. She'd met Joe when she was only twelve; he'd lived close to the house they'd rented when Charlotte's father was alive. He – Joe – had his own market stall and he had *prospects.* He'd promised to marry Charlotte as soon as he had his own shop.

When the boys had gone from the house that morning, Charlotte retrieved the ready-cut cotton shirt parts from the box where her mother had kept them, laid one set of pieces on the floor and tried to fit them together. She found it very difficult: the sewing up of seams, the fitting-in of sleeves and the lining up of yokes and collars was neither so easy nor straightforward as she'd thought, and she was nowhere near as quick and adept as her mother had been. When the boys returned home at six o'clock, she'd not even managed to complete one shirt.

George and Albert had not done well either. Because Albert had been away from work for more than a week, the dog-duffer had found another lad to go out pup-hunting with and Albert was out of a job. He'd spent the day, therefore, looking for cigar-butts with George. Neither had had much success. It had been pouring with rain so there had been very few gentlemen on the street and even fewer discarding their cigar butts, so all they received for their small collection of ends was two pennies, and with these Charlotte bought three medium-sized cooked potatoes for supper.

The following day was not much better. Charlotte ran out of thread and had to pawn an old petticoat of her mother's to enable her to buy two new spools of cotton, and then found it necessary (it was still raining, and very dark) to buy a candle to enable her to see what she was doing. Even in a better light, however, she could not make sense of the cut-out shapes or decide which bit went where, and the pieces kept puckering and fraying instead of going together tidily. Twice she sewed the seams wrongly so they had to be unpicked and sewn again, and when she eventually finished the shirt on the afternoon of the third day, it looked worn and dishevelled. She surveyed it with some dismay: her ma's work had been so neat that the stitches might have been done by a fairy! How could *she* be such a ham-fisted and clumsy worker?

Nevertheless, knowing that unless she got some money they couldn't eat that evening, she smoothed the shirt as best she could, folded it and straightened the collar, then washed her face and brushed her hair ready to take it back to Tommo, the overseer who supplied all the shirt materials to his outworkers and paid them for the finished product.

Tommo didn't live in the higgledy-piggledy, rat-infested slums down by the river like Charlotte, but had a much more respectable address near Haymarket. Charlotte had known of Tommo since she was four years old – when her ma had started working for him – but had not seen him for several years. Since she'd reached a certain age, her ma, for some reason, had preferred to collect the materials and deliver the completed shirts on her own.

The rain finally stopped as Charlotte went out, and she found herself becoming a little more cheerful. Very well, she thought, she *was* pitifully slow at putting a shirt together and – now that she was actually doing it – she realised she loathed sewing, but surely things would improve as she became more competent? Her ma had earned six pennies for each completed shirt, so if she could finish one a day, this would bring in three shillings a week. She'd have to buy thread and shirt buttons out of this, of course, and candles enough to work by, but what she earned, together with any small amount that might be brought in by Albert or George, should be enough to live on. Until Joe came for her...

The streets around Piccadilly were, as usual, teeming with people, for this area was where most of the music and dance halls were, and by early evening sandwich-sellers and hot-pie men were gathering, together with jugglers, magicians and every sort of con man. The prostitutes were the main draw in the area, of course, and Charlotte could not help but be horribly fascinated by the sight of them walking arm-in-arm, flower-hatted and fur-tippetted, taking the air before their regular business hours commenced. She looked through an open front door at two or three young women gathered within, in various stages of undress. A suited city gent passed by and one of the women called out something crude and beckoned him in, but Charlotte was too shy to look back and see whether he'd accepted the invitation. At another house, a girl dressed in electric-blue silk stood at an open door giving out business cards to likely looking men, and yet another young woman, with rouged cheeks, sat astride a wooden crate, her gown pulled above her knees. Charlotte felt herself becoming embarrassed for them; did these girls have no shame?

Tommo lived over the shop, occupying the whole of an imposing house that had tall windows and was fronted by marble columns. One of the rooms downstairs was filled with cutting machines, another was where the finished shirts were delivered, packaged and sent out to the shops. Tommo sat in the first of these rooms, behind a desk, wearing a pin-striped suit and silk shirt. Charlotte remembered him immediately, for he had a large, puckered scar right down one side of his face where, legend had it, a disgruntled worker had once thrown a red-hot iron at him. He did not recognise Charlotte, however.

'Want work, do you?' he said. 'Go and see Bill next door.'

Charlotte shook her head. 'I already work for you,' she said. 'At least, my mother did. Mrs Anderson,' she added.

Tommo started back in surprise. 'I knew she'd copped it,' he said, 'an' I knew she 'ad a daughter to carry on, but I never knew she'd turned out a beauty.'

Charlotte blushed. 'I wonder... wondered if it would be all right to carry on with what Ma was doing,' she said, stumbling over her words. 'I've got enough materials at home to make about ten shirts.'

'If you think you're up to it. If you can work as well as your ma,' Tommo said. He stepped back from Charlotte to look her up and down, then gave a wink. 'But I think you're a bit too decorative to be a-sewing in the rookeries.'

For a moment, Charlotte didn't get his meaning. He rose from the desk, came nearer and put his face very close to hers – so close that she could smell the raw onion he'd eaten for his dinner. 'You, my sweet, are pretty enough to be in one of Tommo's cat-houses. What d'you say to that?'

Charlotte gasped with shock and did not say anything. She could never be like those prostitutes out there. She stared at the floor, waiting for her cheeks to stop burning before she spoke. 'I'll carry on as my mother did, shall I?' she said. 'I'll bring in the shirts next week.' She hesitated; she really needed money for supper. 'I have one shirt here...'

'Don't bring me no singles,' said Tommo. 'Bring me a dozen and you'll get your money.'

Charlotte's face fell. The rent was due and unless the boys had done exceptionally well on the streets, there would be nothing to eat that night.

Tommo came closer. 'But, tell you what, I'll do you a special deal. You give me the shirt and a kiss, and I'll give you a shilling.'

'A kiss?' Charlotte took a step backwards. 'I beg your pardon, but I could not.'

'Oh, hoity-toity, are we? Think you're too good for Tommo?'

Charlotte shook her head wordlessly and backed away.

'Come on – one quick kiss and you'll be on your way with a shilling in your hand.'

Charlotte steadied her breathing. *One shilling. In her hand.* Surely it was worth it? If she refused, he might well shake open the folded shirt, discover how badly it was sewn and decide she shouldn't be paid at all.

'Very well, then,' she said, but so quietly that he had to ask her to repeat it. 'Very well,' she said again, and proffered her cheek.

Ignoring this, he pulled her towards him and pressed his lips straight onto hers, grinding his mouth down so heavily that she felt his teeth cutting into her top lip.

She broke away, feeling frightened and suffocated. Joe had kissed her once, in the park on May Day, but it had not been like that. 'May I have my shilling, please?' she asked, and her voice trembled as she spoke.

He took a coin from his pocket, flicked it into the air and caught it with his other hand. As he offered it to Charlotte he said, 'Double or quits.'

She shook her head.

'Go on. I get another kiss – and a squeeze – and you get an extra shilling. More than fair, that is.'

'No, thank you.' Charlotte backed away, alarmed at what had gone before and ready to forget about the shilling she'd already earned. When she reached the doorway, however, he threw the coin after her. It fell to the floor and, after a moment's hesitation, she bent down and picked it up.

She did not look at the prostitutes when she passed them on her way home.

Reaching St Giles Lane, Charlotte met Mrs Kyle and fell into step beside her. The older girl asked how she was faring.

'We are… *managing*,' Charlotte said after a moment.

Mrs Kyle sighed. 'As are we all. 'Tis a fine balance, is it not, between managing and starving?'

Charlotte nodded wryly.

'But you're a pretty girl, and maybe you'll find a man to look after you.'

'I have a sweetheart,' Charlotte said eagerly. 'I don't see him very often but we have an understanding.'

'Someone who has promised to marry you?' Mrs Kyle asked.

Charlotte hesitated and then fell to doubting. 'He *said* he would, but of course we were very young then. Perhaps he was only jesting.'

She had looked for Joe, of course, sent messages, but he hadn't responded. Perhaps he didn't care any more; perhaps he had married someone else.

'Indeed. Men will promise that sometimes just to have their way with you.'

Charlotte blushed. 'Oh, he did not... I would not... never.'

'Quite right,' said Mrs Kyle. 'Your maidenhead is the most precious possession you own. You must keep it for the man you marry.'

As the week went on, Charlotte worked on the shirts every day from early in the morning until late at night, but by Saturday afternoon she had only completed two more – and they looked very shabby indeed. Her back ached from sitting on a stool and being bent over all day. Her eyes stung and she felt quite weak from lack of food, for the boys had only earned a penny the previous day and the small loaf she'd purchased with this hadn't gone very far between the three of them.

She decided she would send George to Tommo with the two shirts and ask, very humbly, if he could possibly let her have some money for them.

'You're to call him *sir* and be very polite, and say your sister says sorry that there aren't more, but she is working as quickly as she can and will let him have more next week,' Charlotte said, folding the shirts into an old basket. 'Have you got that?'

George repeated her words. 'But why don't *you* go?'

'Just because,' said Charlotte, and looked at him so hard that he didn't dare ask any more questions.

An hour later, George was back, the shirts still in the basket. 'He wants to see you. He says he doesn't do business with little boys,' he reported, frowning deeply at the insult.

Charlotte nodded and sighed. It was as she'd thought it would be.

'Are you going, then?'

Charlotte didn't reply. Instead of going to Tommo, however, she walked along to the street market in The Cut, and by hanging about until most of the stalls were empty, she managed to get some vegetable scraps. Boiled up in a saucepan on the landlady's fire, these made enough thin soup to last three days and put off the meeting she so dreaded.

The weather grew worse. They had no coal and it was so icy in their room that Charlotte's fingers could hardly function well enough to hold a needle and push it through the shirt material. She would do two stitches and then sit shivering, her hands tucked into her armpits in order to warm them enough to do a third. The boys earned pennies here and there: holding horses for gentlemen while they made social calls, carrying parcels for ladies, running alongside carriages turning somersaults in order to amuse those inside. Another week passed, very little money was earned and the rent was overdue. The landlady (who wanted them out of the room so she could put in a larger family and charge more) began talking to Charlotte about the advantages of orphanages, which, she said, although brutal, at least saw to it that children were fed at regular intervals.

Having painstakingly finished another shirt, Charlotte knew that she'd have to go and face Tommo herself, and making herself as warm as possible against the bitter weather, set off. She would call upon his better nature, she decided, implore him to respect her age and innocence. She would ask him to treat her as he would wish his sister treated.

'I don't have a sister,' Tommo said in answer to the little speech she'd given. He gave an unpleasant smile. 'That's fixed you, eh?'

'But if you did have one,' Charlotte stammered, 'perhaps you'd like her treated with respect . . . like a lady.'

'If I had a sister she'd *be* a lady. Not like you,' he said. 'Born in the streets and for the streets, you are.'

Charlotte struggled not to cry while Tommo reached into the basket, pulled out one of the shirts she'd sewn and began to examine it.

'Not very good, are you?'

Charlotte shook her head. 'But I'm sure I'll become better as I go along.' She pointed to the basket and said in as business-like a way as possible, 'There are three shirts here. I wondered if you could possibly see your way to paying me for them.'

'As I said before, I'll give the money when you deliver the goods,' Tommo said. 'All the goods.' His eyes were bloodshot and the cold had emphasised the scar on his cheek so that it looked raw and red.

'I *will* deliver them – it's just that I can't work as quickly as my mother did. The next ones will be better.'

He eyed her up and down. 'Why bother with *them*? Your talents lie elsewhere.'

Charlotte lowered her eyes. Standing in front of him, she felt naked.

'Come and work for me in my cat-house. It's your only hope. I'll find you some nice gentlemen . . . '

She shook her head and backed away. 'I couldn't possibly.' She wanted to say that she was saving herself for Joe, who would surely come for her soon, but she knew Tommo would have laughed. Besides, she had misgivings about Joe since speaking to Mrs Kyle: why hadn't he come for her already? 'I beg you, Mr . . . Mr

Tommo, please behave towards me as you would behave to . . . '

He moved closer and slipped an arm around her waist. 'No need to be nervous,' he said. 'I'll show you what to do.' With his free hand he traced the shape of her body from neck to waist. 'Such a sweet little pigeon . . . '

'No!' said Charlotte, wriggling away.

He made a grab for her, tearing her skirt. Charlotte dropped the basket containing the shirts, dodged around the big cutting machines and ran for the door.

'See you next time!' came the call from behind her.

Charlotte ran into the street. There wouldn't be a next time! She'd find some other way of making money. She'd buy a broom and sweep pathways, mind other people's babies or sell bootlaces from a tray – anything rather than go back and be compromised.

—

December came. A pane of glass in the window of their room got broken and the landlady blamed Albert and refused to replace it. Charlotte found some cardboard to cover the hole and keep out the wind, but that meant that the room was in almost total darkness, needing candles day and night. Even with this extra expense they were just about managing with what the boys brought in, but then came a small catastrophe: George got stuck in some mud while hunting for wood on the foreshore, fell out of his only pair of shoes and quick as a flash someone came up behind him, pulled the shoes out of the mud and ran off with them. By the time George got home his feet were swollen and blue with cold, and Charlotte had to wrap them in rags to try and warm them.

Worried about her brother, Charlotte spent a sleepless night, and early next morning went to a second-hand shop with the only things she had of value: the unused shirt materials belonging to Tommo. By pleading with the man behind the counter (who knew they didn't really belong to her) she managed to obtain the sum of two shillings, and immediately spent one of these on a sturdy pair of boots for George. These were much too large for him (they would still, she hoped, fit when he was twelve) so she stuffed them with newspaper. With the other shilling she paid the rent that was owing.

The following week she hit upon a new way of earning money: she began to beg flowers from the porters at Covent Garden market, wire them onto pins and sell them to gentlemen for their buttonholes. She was out selling these, fortunately, when Tommo paid a visit to their room, having been tipped off by someone that his shirt materials were for sale in a second-hand shop.

'He shouted at me all horrible-like,' George reported to her later, his small frame shuddering with fear. 'He screwed up his face and put it right close to mine and *roared*.'

'It'll be all right. He's gone now,' Charlotte said, and she picked up George and sat him on her knee to comfort him. 'But what did he say?'

'He said he knows what you done, and you needn't think you can sell his 'terials and get away with it. He said he'll come after you again, you see if he don't.'

Charlotte, feeling quite faint with fear, strove to sound normal. 'Anything else?'

George nodded. 'He said he'd take something from us in exchange, but when he looked round the room he said that we lived like cockroaches and there was nothing a decent person would want.'

Charlotte, hearing this, began to weep. It had not always been so. When her father had been alive they'd lived in three large rooms in a respectable house overlooking a park. It had only been after his death that they'd grown so poor.

George looked at her, alarmed. 'Why are you crying?' he asked, but Charlotte just shook her head.

Frightened that Tommo would come looking for her, she took to going to Covent Garden market very early, while it was still dark, and walking into the City to sell her buttonholes. She scuttled there and back along the dark alleyways and stinking backwaters with a blanket over her head so she wouldn't be recognised. Once they were all safely indoors at night, she pushed the mattress up against the door so that no one could get in. She slept fitfully, waking immediately if there were any noises outside.

Two weeks went by and nothing happened, so that Charlotte began to wonder if Tommo had miraculously forgotten all about her. She told Mrs Kyle about her encounters with him, about the kiss she'd sold for a shilling, and said – laughing nervously – that she hoped the world would not condemn her for such a thing.

Mrs Kyle said Charlotte must take care. ''Tis all too easy to be persuaded into first a kiss, then a clasp, then an undoing of your buttons . . . and before you know it, the man has seized his advantage and there you are: a fallen woman.'

Charlotte nodded. Her ma had told her much the same thing.

'Once a woman is fallen she is outside the bounds of society,' Mrs Kyle went on. 'There's a line between rich and poor, you know, and another – a more insurmountable line – between those who are respectable and those who are not. In spite of the poor life I lead, in spite of my miserable circumstances, I have a ring on my finger and so am classed as respectable. A fallen woman can never be that. No decent man would ever want to marry her.'

Charlotte listened and nodded. She already knew all that; it was what every Victorian girl learned from the cradle onwards.

That night, Charlotte had a dream about Joe. They were in the park again, sharing a kiss, which went on for long and tender moments. Then Joe picked her up and carried her through the trees to a flower-strewn glade where he gently laid her on the ground. The sun was shining, there was no one around, and they took off all their clothing without embarrassment or shame. Joe told her she was beautiful, kissed her all over her body until she sighed with pleasure, and then moved on top of her. Charlotte knew that *something* was about to happen – the something that unmarried girls were not supposed to do – but it wasn't a bad or fearful thing, but wonderful and pleasurable and extraordinary. And then a noise in the street woke her and she lay for a long moment feeling sad and bereft, longing to experience those kisses on her body once more.

George's accident happened later that day.

He'd hitched a lift on the back of a gig taking a titled gentleman home after a night of debauchery. When the horse that was drawing the carriage had reared at a barking dog, the carriage had rocked, George had fallen off the back and one of the vast iron wheels had run over his leg.

The accident happened not far from home, luckily, so Albert was able to carry him back to their room.

Here they waited until nearly three o'clock in the afternoon when Charlotte, having sold her flowers, arrived home. By this time, George was slipping in and out of consciousness and Albert was sobbing in terror.

Charlotte, knowing that George was too badly hurt to stand in a queue with scores of others waiting for entry to the Casual Ward at the hospital, ran pell-mell to nearby Harley Street where private doctors were to be found. Getting access to one of these and swearing on her life that she'd be able to pay his bill, she persuaded him to come home with her.

The doctor sighed with dismay as he was led through the slums and gave a shudder of disapproval as he saw the house where they lived, but nevertheless cleaned the wound, stitched it, and applied a bandage which he said would need changing every day for a week. He said that if the limb should prove to be broken, however, then amputation would be the only solution. He would return the following day at the same time, and wanted payment of one shilling for every day he had to attend. He instructed that George should be given nourishing food – plenty of meat – to help the wound heal more quickly.

Charlotte listened to all this, cried a little, then sent Albert to the market with what remained of their money, telling him that he was to buy George the largest meat pie he could find and have one for himself. Then she brushed her hair, tied the blanket tightly round her and went out.

It was approaching evening, and in the wide thoroughfare of Haymarket there was, as before, an atmosphere of jolly, false camaraderie: the well-dressed and well-connected mixing with showmen, beggars, con men and scantily dressed women. This time, however, Charlotte found herself looking beyond the big houses that fronted the road and into the cobbled back alleys and byways, mired with mud and filth, where she caught glimpses of those other young women who, having failed to attract rich admirers, merely catered for any street beggar who came by with a couple of pennies in his pocket. She saw women with ragged, frowsty clothes; matted hair and darkly shadowed eyes, and began to tremble.

Nevertheless, she went into Tommo's premises, asked to see him, and was shown into a back room.

A cynical smile passed across Tommo's face when he saw her. 'Ho! Look who it is! Decided to become one of Tommo's working gels, have you?'

Charlotte clutched the blanket and spoke with as much self-assurance as she could. 'I would not be here, but my little brother had an accident and . . . '

'Little brother, new gown, flowered hat – every girl has her price,' said Tommo.

'I just want to work for a week or two and earn enough to pay for the doctor.'

Tommo began laughing. 'I don't take no part-timers. If I set you up in a place with a decent gown or two, then I own you. Until such time as I decide you're past your best, that is.'

Charlotte hesitated, just for a moment, then thought of little George and asked in a voice that trembled, 'Where shall I go . . . what must I do first?'

'First?' Tommo said. 'First you must pay off the considerable sum of six shillings for the shirt materials that you owe me.' And so saying, he came round the desk and tugged at the blanket she was clutching around her.

Charlotte closed her eyes and tried to stem the wave of nausea that gripped her. There would be no Joe for her now, she knew that, no decent man at all. And as the blanket fell from her shoulders, it seemed that all her future hopes and dreams fell away with it.

THE WAY IT IS

Sophie McKenzie

THE WAY IT IS

Mum and Dad were having a row downstairs. Didn't sound like anything major. I couldn't even hear what they were arguing about, just that Mum was getting all shrill and Dad had started grunting, which he does when he wants her to shut up but doesn't have the balls to turn round and tell her to stop nagging him.

I didn't care.

Doing it with Katya was all I could think about. We'd been together for a few weeks. She'd let me touch her everywhere – I was looking at a picture of her tits saved on my phone right now, in fact – but we hadn't actually shagged.

The truth was that I hadn't shagged anyone.

Ever.

I'd pretended I had, and it had almost happened a few times... But not quite.

Not yet.

That was all changing tonight – with Katya.

At least I was ninety-nine per cent certain it was.

'Sam?' Dad knocked on my bedroom door, then peered round.

'What?' I said, speedily pulling the duvet over my lap and shoving my phone under my pillow.

'Dude, we've got to talk.' Dad sidled into the room, not meeting my eyes.

Oh, great. I stared at him. Was I in trouble? 'Why?'

'This wasn't my idea.' Dad sighed. 'But your mother thinks I should talk to you about... er, stuff.'

Oh. There was an awkward pause while Dad positioned himself at the end of my bed. He stared down at the floor. He's a builder, my dad. Plays guitar in a band with his mates at the weekend. He's got long, shaggy, rock-star hair that starts just a little too high up on his forehead. He also smokes weed every now and then, though Mum makes him go into the garden to do it and I'm not supposed to know.

'Stuff?' I said.

'Yeah, dude...' Dad frowned. He likes to think he's 'down with the kids'. To be honest, I'm beginning to suspect he's a bit of a loser.

We sat side-by-side on the bed. Considering I'm an only child, my room's tiny. That's because my parents can only afford a small house. There's just space for a wardrobe, a chest of drawers and a single bed.

'OK, this is a bit awkward.' Dad glanced at me. 'Er, look at your toes.'

I looked down at my bare feet. Jesus, my right big toe had a wiry black hair growing out of it. When did that get there? Katya says all boys have gross feet. I'd never thought about it before. *Her* feet are small and pretty, like the rest of her. I mentally worked my way up her body… short, slim legs… curvy—

'Sam.' Dad's voice brought me back to the bedroom. I pressed my feet into the wooden floor, searching for the creak that I knew was there. There were several dotted around the room. Dad had laid the floorboards himself and it had been a rush job. That's what he'd said, anyway, justifying the creaks to Mum.

'What?' I was beginning to get irritated now. 'Spit it out, Dad.'

'OK.' Dad shook himself. 'It's about this girl you've been seeing. Katya. About the *physical* side of things.'

What did that mean? Surely. Please, God, surely Dad wasn't trying to give me some sort of sex ed. lecture? It was bad enough doing that sort of thing in PHSE.

I glanced up. Dad caught my eye for a second. His face was bright red. 'I told you, don't look at me, dude,' he said. 'Look at your toes.'

I looked down again, my own face burning now.

'We know you've been going out with her for a few weeks and . . . and there are other girls too. I mean, *course* there are.' I could hear the embarrassed grin in Dad's voice. 'You're *my* son, after all . . . '

Jesus Christ, could he be more of an idiot?

'Anyway,' Dad went on, 'Mum and I . . . well, it was Mum's idea. We think it's time I had *The Talk* with you . . . '

'You're a bit late, Dad,' I said. 'We did all that at school years ago.'

Dad cleared his throat. 'I don't mean the nuts and bolts of it. I know you know about that. I mean, how you . . . how you deal with the situation. With the girl. Things to remember.'

Things to remember? If the situation I was in hadn't been so awkward I'd have smiled. As far as I was concerned, there was just one thing to remember about having sex – where to put your dick. And I didn't think I was going to have any trouble remembering that.

'The most important thing to say is that we . . . *I* . . . am not encouraging you to go out and *do* it,' Dad said. 'But your mum and I realise that you're getting to an age where at some point – maybe not for a year or so, but sooner or later – the situation's going to arise and we want you to be prepared.'

I fixed my gaze on the knot in the wood by my

little toe. Did Mum and Dad somehow know what Katya and I were planning tonight? *No*.

Dad took a deep breath. 'There are several things,' he said. 'To start with you'll need these.' He threw a small packet into my lap.

I glanced at the blue shiny wrapping. Condoms. What kind of moron did Dad think I was? I already had a stash of these. In fact, I'd been carrying one around in my wallet for the past six months.

'These are not a reason to start shagging around, dude,' Dad said. 'But the last thing I want is some girl's father breaking down the door because you've got his little princess up the duff.'

I stared at the floor again, wondering how much more of this I was going to have to put up with.

'OK, so there's the mechanics and the condoms, which are the practical side of things. Then there's the emotional aspect.'

'What?' I looked at him. What on earth was he on about now?

'Sex for the girl is different,' he said. 'Seriously, dude, I've been everywhere and done everything and I can honestly tell you that it doesn't matter how cool or tough she seems, for girls sex is *always* an emotional thing as well as... er... So when the time comes, whenever you *and she* are ready, you need to remember that she's going to need more time before to... to deal with what's happening.'

OK, now I was confused. Was he talking about foreplay? I knew all about *that*, for God's sake. The whole of my life since I was thirteen had been foreplay as far as I was concerned.

'Right, man, that's it.' Dad sounded relieved. 'Any questions?'

I thought about saying: *Yes, why are you such a tit?*

But instead I shrugged.

Dad got up. 'Well, good,' he said. 'Remember I'm here if you want to talk.'

'Right.'

He left and I sighed with relief. There really are some things your parents should stay out of.

Half an hour later I came downstairs, Dad's conversation forgotten, thanks to the prospect of the evening ahead. I was going to a party held by some girl from Katya's school.

Katya. I'd met her one afternoon a few weeks ago at the outdoor swimming pool – the lido. I'd been pissed off cos I was grounded that night. She'd been wearing a red bikini and the sight of her body inside it had given me a hard on that wouldn't go away, even after I went to the toilet and got rid of it . . . twice.

I stood by the front door, hand outstretched, reaching for my keys, remembering. Katya had been with her friends and I'd been with mine and some of them knew each other so it was easy to get talking. Easier, in fact, after she put a dress on over the bikini.

It took about five minutes for me to decide I was going to ignore the fact that I was grounded that night, which later got me grounded twice more, but I didn't care.

Katya and I went out with some of the other people at the lido, but we both soon forgot about everyone else. It wasn't just the body under the bikini. She was fun. I liked the way her green eyes slanted when she laughed. I liked how easy it was to talk to her. How we liked the same music. We talked and danced and got drunk. She didn't want an E so I didn't do one either. She told me about her life and her over-protective Polish mum and how her dad had died when she was six (which was obviously awful, but on the other hand, did mean I could give her a hug and feel her tits through my T-shirt), and how she liked cats but was scared of horses. And I liked her. I really did. But, in the end, all I could think about was that body, under that bikini, under that dress.

Later, I'd walked her home and we'd sneaked into the park and I'd taken her dress off. And she'd let me put my hand where it had wanted to be all night.

That had happened three or four times since then. And now it was tonight. And Katya would be at the party. And she'd said she was ready to shag me. At least I was ninety-nine per cent sure she had.

Me and that body.

I shook myself as I came to, still standing by the front door reaching for my keys. As my fingers curled round the metal I heard Dad in the kitchen.

'I honestly don't think we've got anything to worry about,' he was saying wearily. 'He just looked embarrassed, and you know how open we've always been with him. I honestly think he would say if there was an issue with anything.'

'Never mind "an issue",' Mum snapped back. 'Now he's got some sort of girlfriend, is he likely to be sexually active in the near future?'

Dad sighed, then grunted. 'I'm sure he isn't. He looked at the condoms I gave him like they were artefacts from outer space. I'm sure he's thinking about it a lot, but I don't think he's got much idea of what it... you know... actually involves .'

Yeah, right, Dad.

Grinning, I grabbed my keys and headed on into the night.

Jade and I stood side-by-side in the bathroom, doing our make-up.

'So, Katya... tell me about Sam,' she said.

I picked up a pot of green, glittery eye shadow and smiled into the mirror. 'He's like really fit.'

'Fitter than Zac Efron?' Jade frowned at my reflection, as if the thought were impossible to get her head round.

I glared at her. 'How old are you?' I said. 'And, yes, way fitter than bloody Zac Efron.'

Jade shook her head. She'd had a massive crush on Zac Efron for, like, six million years – long after the rest of us had all grown out of it.

It wasn't the only annoying thing about her.

Jade reached for her lip gloss while I dabbed the brush into the eye shadow. Soon we would leave my house and walk round the corner to the party.

Where I would see Sam.

I stroked the green, glittery eye shadow across my eyelid. Jade was applying some bright orange lip gloss. It wouldn't have suited most people – but against her dark skin it looked fantastic.

I studied my reflection. Too short. Too fat. Too ugly. Especially my face. My eyes are green – I guess they're OK. But my hair's thin and lank and this horrible dirty mouse colour. I'd love blonde highlights. I think they'd make my hair look a million times better, which would make me feel a million times better. But of course Mum won't let me have highlights, just like she won't let me have a tattoo. I'd like one of a heart inside a circle, or maybe a star or a dolphin – you know, something classic. Mum won't even let me get my ears pierced! I mean, you'd have thought she'd have learned her lesson after Marta – that's my older sister – got pregnant last year. There's no point being ultra-strict. Your kids are going to do what they want anyway.

That's just the way it is.

'You look good, Kat,' Jade said with a smile.

'Yeah? What d'you want?'

'Can I borrow that black top of yours?'

'Sure. I'm wearing the green anyway.'

We made our way back to my bedroom. It's huge – it used to be Mum and Dad's, before Dad died. Mum moved into the spare room soon after that and has stayed there. Marta slept here before she got pregnant. Mum was so mad at first she wouldn't have her in the house, but then Marta moved back and Tommy was born and they took over what used to be the dining room downstairs. Marta says she likes being down there on her own. Plus there's a shower room, so she's got, like, her own private bathroom, which is cool.

'Sam's not just fit,' I said, pulling on my jeans. 'He's really sweet too.'

'You mean sweet as in romantic? Like, giving you flowers?'

'More . . . I dunno . . . like, sensitive. You know, like when I told him about my dad he gave me this big hug and was really sympathetic about it.'

'Right.' Jade nodded approvingly. 'That's nice. Has he bought you anything?'

I stared at her. She'd slipped on my black top. It was baggy on her, hanging loosely off one shoulder. She looked like a supermodel.

'You mean, like jewellery?' I said, uncertainly.

'No, you idiot, like drinks and meals and going to the cinema.'

'Yeah,' I said, picking up the green top. 'Well, drinks and stuff. We've only been out once properly, apart from the first time we met and that other time when we bumped into each other.'

'Ooh, like fate.' Jade grinned.

'Yeah, I guess.' I shrugged, not wanting to sound too loved-up. The truth was that I had thought the way we'd bumped into each other was fate. But then, I'd thought it was fate from the moment I'd seen him. There was just something about the way he looked: that slightly aloof way he slouched along – and the way his eyes melted you when he looked at you.

That's why I'd said yes to tonight. To seeing him. Why I'd hinted I'd go the whole way with him. Make love.

Properly.

It would be my first time. His too, I was guessing from the way he hadn't pushed me too hard before. Guys who are used to shagging tend to expect it. But not Sam. It was one of the things I liked about him.

I slipped on the green top. It was sleeveless and low cut, with a line of sequins across the front.

I turned sideways on, checking myself out.

'You look great, Kat,' Jade said.

Maybe. I still hated my arse and thighs, even in these jeans. But the top, I had to admit, did look good, particularly the way it hid my tummy.

I pulled it off and shoved it into a plastic bag, along with the high-heeled sandals I'd bought last week with some of my birthday money. I loved those sandals – they were green and silver, with the highest heels I'd ever owned.

Beautiful.

Plus they had open toes and Sam had said he thought I had pretty feet. Maybe they'd draw his attention away from my fat butt.

I yanked a jumper off my cupboard shelf and pushed it into the plastic bag, on top of the other things. Then I took a brown, polo-neck cotton jumper out of my drawer and dragged it over my head.

'What are you doing?' Jade stared at me, open-mouthed.

I grinned. 'Getting past Mum.'

Jade nodded. 'So how far have you gone with this Sam?' she said.

'Everything but,' I said. 'He's a really good kisser.'

'Have you sucked his dick?' Jade giggled.

'Course.'

I hadn't really. To be honest I hadn't fancied the idea of it much. They're not exactly attractive, boys' bits. Not that I'd seen many. Sam had put my hand on his thing the last time we'd been together. He'd groaned when I rubbed it up and down. I liked him doing that, it made me feel – I dunno – like he was in my power or something. But the touching itself was a bit boring. Both ways – in fact. I mean, what's so great about having your boobs kneaded like dough and someone jabbing a finger inside you?

I preferred it when he kissed me. Like I said, his kissing was great. It made my whole body tingle.

'So you gonna do it tonight?' Jade went on, her eyes wide.

'Might do,' I said. 'See how I feel, I guess.'

Jade nodded. Inside I was suddenly grabbed with anxiety. Suppose Sam had gone off the whole idea? Suppose there was somebody else at the party he liked better?

That wouldn't just be humiliating. It would hurt.

'I'm not being a slag, you know,' I said, putting on my trainers. 'I really like him.'

'I know, babe,' Jade said soothingly. 'Anyway, you're only a slag if you do, like, random guys, like Laura Atkins. Everyone knows that.'

We made our way downstairs. Mum appeared in the kitchen doorway as we reached the bottom of the stairs. She had Tommy in her arms and looked slightly flushed, her fine hair escaping from her hideous black-velvet scrunchy.

'Can you take him for a bit, Katya?' she asked. 'Marta's phoned to say she's got to stay on a bit at work and I'm trying to scrub the oven.'

I made a face. Like the oven needed scrubbing! Everything in our house is in a state of high cleanliness at all times. I sometimes wonder if Mum worries there's some kind of Housekeeping Gestapo likely to check up on her washing and tidying abilities at any moment.

'I can't, Mum. We're going to that party I told you about. If we don't go now we'll be late.'

Mum frowned. She looked me up and down, taking in the brown polo-neck top and the trainers. 'OK. Whose party is it?'

I bit my lip, trying to keep my temper. 'I told you last week. It's at Danielle's house from school. Just round the corner.'

Mum nodded distractedly. 'And her parents are there?'

'God, Mum, everybody goes to parties now where the parents are out, but yes,' I lied, 'her parents will be in. You've met them at school. And I'm staying over at Jade's after. Remember?'

'And your parents are in tonight too, Jade?'

Jade nodded, knowing her lines. 'They're expecting us back by eleven. My dad's going to walk round to pick us up. He's very protective.'

This was all a total lie. Jade's dad was always in the pub and pissed by eleven on a Saturday night. Anyway, Jade had told her parents that she was staying over with me.

Excitement surged through me. We were free to stay at the party – or go wherever we wanted – for as long as we liked.

Tommy gurgled and waved a chubby foot at me. I reached over and he curled his tiny, perfect toes round my fingernail.

'He's sooo cute,' Jade trilled.

'Mmm.' Mum pursed her lips.

'We gotta go, Mum,' I said, edging towards the door.

'All right.' She absently brushed her hair out of her eyes, leaving a grimy smear across her cheek. 'Have you got your phone?'

'Yes.'

'Is it charged and switched on?'

'Yes, Mum.' I reached for the door handle.

'It'll be cold later…'

'I've got a jumper with me.' I held out the plastic bag.

Mum nodded approvingly. Beside me, Jade stifled a giggle.

'Fine,' Mum said. 'Well, be careful.'

'I will,' I said, and I opened the front door and escaped out into the street.

Free, at last.

My eyes follow her as she walks across the room. Loads of guys are looking at her. Tight jeans. Porn-star heels. Sexy, revealing top. Everything says Katya is up for it. She turns, sees me looking and smiles.

I smile back, fingers curling round the pack of condoms in my pocket. When am I supposed to put one on? Jesus, it's going to be a bit embarrassing stopping and doing it while we're halfway through. I've got to get those jeans off too. Why couldn't she be wearing a skirt? Suppose I fumble with it or break it or something? Maybe I should go to the bog and put one on now.

No. No time. Katya's on her way over, a giggling black girl at her side.

'Hi, Sam, this is Jade.'

I glance at the black girl. She's tall, nearly as tall as me, and actually quite beautiful. But all I can think about is how to get rid of her so I can have Katya to myself.

Luckily, a third girl appears. Neither sexy nor beautiful, she flings her arms round Katya and Jade.

'Hey, guys. It's sooo lovely to see you.' She's slurring. Off her face.

Katya and Jade roll their eyes. 'Godsake, Laura. We saw you yesterday at school,' Katya says.

Laura ignores this. She steps back, swaying. Her eyes widen as she looks me up and down. 'Hi,' she says. 'I'm Laura Atkins.'

'Hi,' I say. The name seems familiar. I'm sure I've heard a couple of boys talking about her at school. 'I think I've heard of you.'

'I'm sure you have.' Jade throws Katya a look I don't understand, giggles, then takes Laura's arm and steers her away.

We're alone. It's hot in here and I'm sweating and the condoms are burning a hole in my pocket.

'D'you want to go outside?' I ask.

Katya nods. As we reach the kitchen – a mess of spilt beer, ransacked fridge and empty bottles – I put my arm round Katya's shoulders. I think about what we're about to do. What it will be like. The skin on her arms is soft and warm. As we squeeze past a couple snogging at the sink, her tits press up against me. I feel the weight of them. The shape of them.

I almost come on the spot. And then I realise Katya is speaking.

'I've got a nephew,' she says. 'His name's Tommy. He's really sweet but you have to watch him all the time now he's crawling.'

'Oh.' I'm still thinking about what we're about to do. My heart's thumping. I can't focus on anything else. This is it. This is totally gonna be it.

My first time.

We wander into the garden. It's warm. I spot a group of people from my school and steer Katya away from them. Past a couple of puke puddles and we reach a line of trees covered in fairy lights. It's quieter here. We move beyond the trees, into the bushes. Other couples are dotted about, but they're barely on my radar.

Katya's staring at me now, as if she expects me to say something. I can't remember what we were talking about.

We stop and stare at each other. 'So, my sister has this little boy,' she says.

I smile, hoping I'm not looking as nervous as I feel. 'Kids are great,' I say.

Before she can speak again, I bend down and kiss her.

It's amazing. But I want more. I'm just wondering if she'll let me move onto her tits, when she draws away from me.

'My mum was a total pain in the arse before I left. She's like *so* unfair. She's like the police or something.

She won't even let me be on Facebook, so I have to do it under a different name.'

'Right. Poor you.' I'm sympathetic. I really am and if she'll just let me do this I promise I'll listen to her all night.

I kiss her again and bring my hands round, under her top.

She doesn't stop me.

Oh, crap, he's undone my bra and he's doing that kneading thing with my boobs. Still, I do like the kissing. Mmm. I really like the kissing. But now he's tugging at my jeans.

'Wait,' I say.

He stops.

'I don't know.' I can feel my face flushing in the cool night air. It's warm out here, but suddenly I shiver. I'd thought I really liked him. But I'm not sure now.

'Don't know what?' he says.

'This,' I say vaguely, waving my hand between the two of us.

Sam smiles. He does have a really cute smile. I waver. Maybe I should just carry on.

It's what he expects. It's what he wants.

It's what I've more or less said we'd do. And yet...

I look down at my green and silver sandals. Even in this light I can see the earth smeared up the sides. Sam doesn't care about my shoes – or Tommy – or my mum turning into one of the Nazis her family ran away from a billion light years ago.

It strikes me that I don't even really know him.

'I'd like it if we had a bit more time,' I stammer. 'Before we go any further.'

'More time? OK.' He sounds bewildered. 'What do you want to do, then . . . get a drink or something?'

I'm feeling really embarrassed now. God this was a bad idea.

'I don't mean more time tonight . . . ' I let the words hang in the air. Across the bush from us comes the sound of ragged, heavy breathing. A boy grunting. A girl moaning. Ooh, yeah, babe. Music drifts out from the house. A steady thump. A dance track. Ooh, yeah, babe.

Maybe we should go inside and just have a dance. But as I look at Sam I know I don't want to dance. Not with him.

It was there. I was ninety-nine per cent certain it was there. But it's gone.

I sigh. 'Sorry,' I say. I tug down my top.

Sam frowns. 'Did I do something?'

What, apart from being a bit useless at petting, as they call it in those ridiculous talks they make you sit through at school?

'You're a good kisser,' I say.

Sam shoves his hands in his pockets. He draws out a small, shiny blue packet. 'I brought condoms.'

'Right.' I waver again, seeing as he's all prepared. And I did kind of say we'd do this. Everyone else has done it. I don't want to be the last person I know that has sex.

Plus Sam is sweet. I mean, he hugged me when I told him about my dad and he likes kids.

He shoves the condoms into his back pocket and pulls me towards him again. Starts kissing. Moves his mouth lower. Onto my neck. Under my top. It starts raining and we sink down into the bushes. The rain is soft and light and warm and it somehow makes the whole thing really sexy. The way his lips slide over my wet skin.

For a while I'm loving it. Loving the way my whole body is sort of glowing. But then it goes on. And on. And he starts prodding at me with his fingers. And my mind wanders and I can hear dance music and I'm wondering what Jade's doing inside and if she's having a better time than me and the ground's cold under my back and I'm wet and he's still going at me with his fingers and there's a stone sticking into my left shoulder blade.

I sit up. The rain stops. Sam's jerky breathing is the only sound in the still air around us. The other couples have gone. Further away are squeals and laughter and music and traffic.

Here, it's just me and him.

I fasten my bra and stand up.

'Katya?' Sam sounds confused.

'You're sweet,' I say. 'I'm sorry.'

A pause as I pull down my top again.

'Are you dumping me?' he says.

I don't know what to say to that. I'm not even sure what the answer is. I just want to get back inside the house and find Jade and have a laugh.

I shrug.

'Right.' Sam folds his arms. 'Thanks.' Now he sounds sarcastic.

I look at him. 'See you around.'

He nods and I walk away. Past the bushes and trees, the ground is soft from the rain. My sandals sink into the earth. I stop and slip them off. I don't want them ruined.

I glance over my shoulder. Sam has wandered over to a group of people on the other side of the garden. He's not looking at me.

I watch for a second and he laughs. One of the girls in the group touches his arm. For a second I feel insanely jealous, like I want to rush back and shout at her to bloody back off and then drag Sam into the bushes and shag him all beautifully and passionately, like it was supposed to be . . . like I was certain I wanted it to be.

But even as I'm thinking it, I know that's not what I really want.

I know he's not what I really want.

I watch some more. He glances in my direction, then turns back to the girl touching his arm. They talk for a moment. He pats his back pocket – where he stashed his condoms.

Does he know I'm still looking?

Or is he just making sure he's still got those condoms?

I can't work it out, but I carry on watching as Sam puts his arm round the girl and leans into her. She smiles up at him and suddenly I don't want to be watching any longer.

I look down at my feet, at where they've sunk into the soft, wet earth.

People are going to do what they want.

That's just the way it is.

The earth around my feet is really squelchy. Mud oozes up, through my toes. I squeeze them together, enjoying the cool squidgy sensation against my skin.

A shriek from the house. Jade is waving at me, all excited, from a window. She points at the boy standing next to her and grins.

I grin back, then pull my feet out of the mud.

Without looking round, I head across the damp earth, towards the house.

THE WHITE TOWEL

Bali Rai

THE WHITE TOWEL

Maisie looked at me like I was nuts.

'Get lost!' she said, stretching out on my bed. We were supposed to be revising for our GCSEs but Maisie had started talking about sex. Again. I swear she was worse than the lads we knew. The lads were immature and unable to control their hormones, so at least they had an excuse. Maisie was just obsessed.

'It's true,' I protested.

'Virgins?' said Maisie.

I nodded.

'It's tradition,' I replied. 'You have to be a virgin on your wedding night. That's why you don't see that many Asian girls putting it about... or pretending to, at least.'

'But what about having fun and trying new things and...' she continued until I shook my head.

'Haven't you heard about "honour killings"?' I asked her.

'Yeah... I'm not dim, Preet.'

I shrugged. 'Well, some girls get attacked for not being virgins; killed even...'

'Rubbish!' my best friend said.

But I knew different...

Dry, ochre-coloured dust burned my nostrils as the pails of creamy water buffalo milk I was carrying grew heavier with each step. I stumbled along the narrow path between my uncle's house and that of his brother, wishing I hadn't volunteered to help with the daily chores. I was on holiday from England. Three long weeks in a Punjabi village; fried by an unrelenting sun and feasted upon by engorged mosquitoes, droning mercilessly in the darkness. I spent each night waiting to get bombed. Each morning I woke up itchy, covered in raw scarlet bumps.

My T-shirt was soaked through; the sky-blue fabric dark with perspiration. My trainers, gleaming white and fresh that morning, were ruined; covered in the red dust and stained by the thick, warm milk that I was spilling everywhere. It was all down my grey combats too. All I could think about was how much I wanted a shower.

Something crawled along my hairline, tickling the hairs with its legs. I wanted to slap whatever it was into oblivion but I couldn't put down the pails. I'd never pick them up again if I did. I thought of my Indian cousins; especially the girls. The ones who worked out in the fields all summer long and never complained. The heat was intense and inescapable, yet they brushed it off with a shrug and a smile. Each of them, though skinny, was strong, much stronger than I'd ever be. My old man was right – me and my sister had it cushy.

'Blinking easy life you got, innit?' he would tell us. 'Everything buy for you an' food on table. Even your bottoms clean for you. Wanna try living in bleedin' India for a week.'

And as my sister and I would protest, he'd chuckle to himself and call us soft. Now I knew that he was right, as I struggled to complete my task.

Suddenly my head grew light and I felt dizzy. My legs gave up; I stumbled and fell, spilling the milk everywhere. My forehead cracked against one of the metal pails and the rim cut through the skin. I turned over onto my back and touched the wound. Blood streamed out: thick, rich and crimson. I lay still for a moment, trying to catch my breath as a cold sweat broke out all over my body. My thoughts were all fuzzy and I began to shiver. An instant fever took hold.

I got up, unsure of my feet for a moment, blinking in the bright light, as a rainbow danced before my eyes. I counted to ten slowly and deliberately, taking in as much air as I could manage. Eventually I steadied myself and staggered towards my uncle's house.

I stumbled into the open courtyard, holding my left hand against the gash in my forehead. My fingers dripped with blood. It streamed down my face and stained my sweaty T-shirt. I felt queasy and fell to my knees, as my stomach lurched. My aunt appeared from the house and ran towards me, holding her hands to her mouth.

'Dear God!' she shouted, in Punjabi, before calling to her husband.

My uncle ran over with a towel and pressed it against the wound.

'What happened?' asked my aunt.

'I don't know,' I replied. My voice was a croak. 'I felt dizzy and then I fell over.'

My uncle took the towel away from the cut and looked at it. It was covered in blood. I focused on my aunt, as I began to see double. I took more deep breaths and tried to clear my head. I saw my aunt glance at the towel and flinch. As my head began to pound, I saw a dark cloud of emotion pass across her face. She looked away from the towel, squeezing one hand into the other. My uncle lifted me to my feet, guiding me slowly towards the house. Once inside, he sat me down on a *manjah*; a bed, made from a wooden frame with interwoven strands of rope acting as the mattress.

'Sohni!' he shouted to one of his sons, 'Preet has hurt herself. Get the doctor quick!'

As my fever grew stronger, the shivers took over. The room began to whirl around me and the voices grew slow and deep. Yet, as I faded, I remember wondering about my aunt's reaction to the towel. It wasn't the sight of my blood that had made her flinch. It was something else; something that saddened her. I wondered what it could have been as I passed out.

Later, as I lay shivering in the heat and humidity, with fever torching its way through my body, I asked my aunt about her reaction.

'To what, *beteh*?' she replied, pretending that she didn't understand.

'The towel.'

She looked away. Another cloud of sadness passed across her face.

'It's nothing,' she told me but I didn't believe her.

'It has to be *something*,' I insisted. 'What is it about that towel?'

She sighed, stood up and walked over to the door, pushing it shut. When she returned and sat by my side, she picked up a damp cloth and wiped the sweat from my forehead, carefully avoiding the wound, which the doctor had cleaned with iodine and then patched up with a dressing. It would need stitches but the local hospital was far away. My uncle had agreed to take me the following morning.

'*Beteh*,' replied my aunt, 'there are things that you don't understand. Things about our family...'

'Such as...?' I asked, wincing a little.

My aunt looked up at the ceiling and then back at me. I could tell that she was unsure of what to say. I was intrigued.

'We had a sister, your father and me,' she began. 'A younger sister called Jagpreet. She was so beautiful and clever and full of joy...'

'The one that went mad and killed herself?' I asked, remembering what my dad had told me about her.

'Yes, only she didn't go mad.'

A fat tear welled in my aunt's eye.

'But my dad said that...' I began.

'He lied,' said my aunt. 'We all lied.'

'Why?' I asked, confused. 'Has this got something to do with the towel?'

My aunt let a few tears fall and then pulled herself together. She looked at the door again, as if to make sure no one was listening. Then she told me this story.

***

Jagpreet was a happy-go-lucky girl with honey-brown hair that looked blonde in the sunlight. She had warm, cream-coloured skin and eyes that shone out like amber stones. She was the kind of girl that every boy in the village wanted to spend time with. Often she would go out into the fields to do her chores for a day and return having done nothing, all her work done for her by lovesick teenagers anxious to catch her eye and her heart. Not that she played on this or took advantage of her suitors. She exuded innocence about such things, my aunt told me. She didn't even notice the admiring looks she received as she walked barefoot around the alleyways and gullies of the village, or washed her hair under the hand pump, the water stretching her clothes across full breasts and wide hips. She just thought that people were being kind to her; that the young men who would have died for her were merely being brotherly.

At the age of fourteen Jagpreet was fully grown. Men from around the village and beyond began to arrive at her father's door, ready to betroth their sons and heirs to her. Once, in just seven days, my aunt told me, thirteen potential fathers-in-law visited and took tea with her father. Thirteen men who wished to see their sons happy. To see their longing satisfied. The beautiful girl they had caught a glimpse of out in the fields or among the mango-tree groves had enchanted them. She was magical, said my aunt.

Everyone loved her and wanted to be her friend, even people she'd met for the first time. Frightened animals calmed when she whispered to them. Babies stopped crying when she looked into their eyes, smiling and stroking their brows. An old lady from the village had seen Jagpreet sleeping out in the fields once, in the shade of a well, and swore on the Ten Gurus that as she slept, a cobra, black as jet and as long as a stream, had slithered past her, caressing her smooth skin before moving on.

Her family adored her. She was the youngest child and the most loved by her father, a stout Jat Sikh; my grandfather. Normally such fatherly adoration was confined to the male heirs of a family. But my grandfather had viewed Jagpreet with the same pride as his only son. My aunt wiped away another tear as she revealed that my grandfather had cried when Jagpreet died. How he'd been left a broken man with nothing but a cold stone, full of grief, where his heart should have been. He had been so broken that he'd died calling out her name, almost a year to the day after her passing.

It was the day that Jagpreet turned sixteen that her short life began to tumble towards its end. She had returned from the fields one afternoon carrying a small bird that had broken its wing, crying at its pain. Her father called to her. She left the bird lying on her soft pillow and made her way out to the courtyard, wiping her eyes. Her father was sitting drinking spiced tea with a tall, distinguished-looking man from a village ten miles to the west, close to the city of Chandigarh. The man was a wealthy trader, a Jat who had earned his wealth selling sumptuous fabrics and whose brother was living in England, working and sending money back to his family. As she approached, the stranger stood and hugged her as if she were his own daughter and proceeded to tell her of his son, Malkit, a much sought-after boy of eighteen years, who was studying to become a teacher.

Jagpreet looked to her father, searching his eyes for an explanation. Her father smiled and called her to him. Taking her hand, he told her that she had been betrothed to Malkit and that the stranger was her father-in-law, a wonderful man from a big, wealthy family. The kind of family that would look after her and love her.

Jagpreet turned to their guest and gave a smile so warm, so loving, that he had to avert his eyes. A tear ran down his cheek. He turned to Jagpreet's father.

'*Bhai-ji*, your daughter is truly as you said; beautiful and so pure. It gladdens my heart to take her as my daughter-in-law.'

'This day has been blessed by the Gurus,' replied Jagpreet's father. 'For today two families have become one.'

The fathers embraced warmly and the guest went on his way, eager to return to his son with the good news. Jagpreet took her father's hand again.

'Father, will you still love me as before?' she asked. 'When I am married and part of another's family?'

'*Beteh*, I could never love you less than I do now, only more. But tell me – are you truly happy with the path that I have chosen for you?'

'Yes,' she told him. 'If you have chosen for me then I must obey. I know you have chosen well.'

'Are you sure, Jagpreet? I would not wish to make you unhappy.'

'Then tell me what this boy is like – Malkit.'

Her father looked away.

'I must confess that I haven't seen him,' he replied. 'But his father is a well-respected man and I trust his words. Malkit, he tells me, is tall and handsome, with skin as light as milk, and strong as an ox. He is studying to be a teacher and he will take you to England when he goes. England, *beteh*, where life is so much easier than it is here.'

Jagpreet smiled.

'He sounds so wonderful,' she said. 'When will we be married?'

'Soon, my love... soon. I will begin organising everything in the morning.'

'May I go and tell my friends?' asked Jagpreet.

'Yes, *beteh*, you may,' laughed her father. 'Today we have been blessed by the Lord. *Waheguru Satnam*.'

My aunt stopped at this point in the story, pausing to wipe her eyes free of tears. If only he had known, she said to me. If only he *could* have known. She swabbed my forehead with a wet towel before she told me the rest of the tale.

The preparations for the wedding began the next day just as my grandfather had said they would. My aunt told me of trips to Chandigarh to buy fine silks and Indian gold. She told me of men coming to the house to take orders for sweetmeats and dhal and rice. Of the hunchback, Mahon Singh, who lived down the gully from our family and who was related to a famous Punjabi folk singer and had asked him to come along. Mahon Singh led a small band of horn players and they were hired to play during the three days of celebration. The wedding would be the best that Jagpreet's father could afford. No one would ever be able to say that he hadn't seen off his beloved daughter in style.

Some of Jagpreet's former suitors became angry at news of the wedding. They began to tell tales about her. Some said that she was not the pure, innocent girl that she seemed. Others lied that they had sullied her honour, her *izzat*, with their ardour. That she was not a virgin. These rumours were dismissed by the majority of the villagers, but the ramblings of disgruntled and jealous men continued until finally, two months after they had begun, everything was ready and the wedding festival began.

It lasted for three days and three nights and the entire village attended, as did many from round about. The two families met each other on the wedding day itself and got on so well that an outsider would have sworn they had known each other for centuries. Jagpreet's mother got on famously with Malkit's mother. His brothers laughed and joked with hers. And so on down the family line. Many chickens and goats were slaughtered to feed the revellers and much homemade corn spirit was consumed. As his fans mobbed him, the folk singer sang of Sohni-Mehiwal and Heer-Ranja – star-crossed lovers from an earlier age – and of the glory of the Punjab, the scarred and beautiful land of five rivers. Such was the fuss that the local police called by. When they took in the scene, they decided to call a holiday, and stayed on as guests.

Eventually the final evening came and it was time for Jagpreet's groom to carry her away to his own village, his entourage, or *juneth*, in tow. First he had to approach the gates of Jagpreet's father's house and ask to be let in. My aunt was weeping openly as she told me this part and I had to sit up and comfort her at one point.

'Oh, *beteh*, Malkit was as handsome as any man I have ever seen. Truly a match for my sister…'

'Please carry on,' I begged, eager to find out what happened after the wedding.

My aunt explained how the women, as is tradition, teased Malkit at the gate and refused to let him pass until he had given them something. At first he offered pennies, then a rupee and then five and ten. Eventually he gave them twenty rupees each and they let him through, all the while teasing him and trying to play tricks on his best man, who was with him. Malkit ignored the jibes and embraced Jagpreet's father, drank from a cup of milk and then asked for his bride. Jagpreet appeared from her room, resplendent in fine crimson-coloured silk, more beautiful than a flower, and drank from the same cup as her husband. Then, as Jagpreet's sister – my aunt – and female cousins began to wail and cry, she bade her family goodbye. She saved the longest embraces for her mother and father, who wept openly at the loss of their daughter to another family, even though it was such a happy occasion.

Finally she made her way to the gate with her brother, my father, walking behind her. It is tradition too that the bride's brother accompany her to her new home on the first night. As she sat in the horse-drawn carriage that would take her to her new life, several of the villagers began to cry too and the children of the village lined the dirt path and waved and smiled, blowing her kisses. One or two of her suitors, minds clouded with opium smoke, stood sullenly with drooping eyes and breaking hearts and watched her go. Jagpreet cried too, said my aunt, yet she smiled as well, for she was happy, excited, sad and afraid all at once. She was leaving all that she had ever known for something new. Who knew when they would see her again or where? She belonged to another family now, said my aunt. It was like a candle being extinguished.

The return to Malkit's village was triumphant and the festivities continued long into the night. Malkit spent his time with friends and family rather than his new bride. He would have to wait for the following night to have her to himself, once she had been prepared and had settled in a little. Malkit's mother and sisters would take care of Jagpreet first, making sure that she was happy and giving her instruction in the ways of married life. It was tradition. Instead Malkit sang, danced and drank with his friends. Late into the night, he collapsed in a dreamy, happy daze, sleeping until the sunrise with a smile across his face.

It was while he and Jagpreet slept that a messenger arrived at Malkit's parents' door – a shabbily dressed man of low standing, barefoot and half-naked. He asked one of Malkit's cousins for Malkit's mother, Naseebo, who was herself still awake and chatting happily with her friends. Naseebo told the cousin to send the messenger packing.

'Is he an *idiot*?' she asked. 'Can he not see that we are in the middle of a wedding?'

'He insists that you come to the gate, *thai-ji*,' replied the cousin.

'Oh, very well, but if he is wasting my time I want you to beat some sense into him, the *chamarr*.'

'Agreed,' said the cousin, following his aunt back to the gate.

The messenger considered Naseebo for a moment before moving in close to whisper to her.

'Tell the boy to leave us,' he said.

'Never!' exclaimed Naseebo in disgust. 'You think that I would drag my *izzat* through the mud? That I'd stand at my *own* gate, in the middle of the night, with a strange man? I would rather cut off my own nose.'

'I am a eunuch, sister,' replied the man, 'and of no threat to your honour. And I fear that someone has *already* cut off your nose.'

Naseebo took stock of the eunuch, realising that he was as he claimed to be. She sent the cousin to stand about ten feet away from the gate before turning back to the messenger.

'Tell me quickly what you mean,' she hissed through narrow lips. 'And if I think you are lying I will have you hanged before the morning.'

The eunuch smiled, showing a set of yellowing and broken teeth.

'*Speak!*' Naseebo hissed.

'Your daughter-in-law is not what she seems,' he told her with a malicious grin.

'You *dare* to besmirch my family's honour...' she began.

'Hear me out, sister,' said the eunuch. 'What use is a flower when its petals are soiled? When its bloom has been taken?' he asked.

Naseebo's breathing quickened.

'What are you telling me, you dog?'

The eunuch grinned yet further.

'You *know* what I say. And you know *how* to see if I am telling the truth,' he said.

'Who are you?' Naseebo asked him.

The eunuch thought about the money he'd been paid to deliver his message.

'I am the person who will save your honour,' he told her. 'Nothing more.'

Naseebo's ebony eyes narrowed. She regarded the eunuch with unconcealed loathing.

'If I find out that you are lying,' she told him, 'my sons will cut out your heart.'

'If I am lying may the Lord strike me down,' replied the eunuch. 'I merely came to pass on this message. You and your kin mean nothing to me...'

And with that he turned and walked off into the night.

Naseebo had to wait until the following night to test the eunuch's story, said my aunt, *after* my father had left. She enlisted one of Malkit's sisters, Gian, in her task, telling no one else. Just before their first night together, Naseebo gave Malkit a brand new white towel and told him to place it underneath Jagpreet as they did their business for the first time.

'It is tradition,' she explained after Malkit had questioned her. 'Nothing more than tradition, my son.'

Meanwhile Gian dealt with Jagpreet, brushing her hair and rubbing coconut oil into her skin. She too told Jagpreet of the white towel and said that it meant nothing.

'Just tradition,' she lied. 'Nothing more...'

As Malkit took his bride to bed for the first time, he closed and locked the door behind them, suspecting nothing.

My aunt stopped again and looked into my eyes.

'Do you understand about the towel?' she asked me.

I wanted to say yes but I couldn't. My headache was getting worse and I felt a little confused. I shook my head.

'There is an old wives' tale,' she explained. 'It says that *all* virgins bleed when they...'

I could see that my aunt was embarrassed so I told her that I understood what she meant.

'Only it isn't true,' my aunt added sadly. 'Not all the time. It just isn't true...'

The story continued. At dawn, Malkit, as requested, brought the towel to his mother who inspected it. Seeing no sign of blood, Naseebo nearly fainted, catching herself at the last moment. Then the anger took over.

'They have cheated us!' she cried, pulling Jagpreet from the bedroom by her hair. She dragged her to the courtyard and threw her, screaming and crying, to the dusty ground.

'WHORE!' she screamed. 'THIEF!'

The family came running as Naseebo's curses shattered the peace of a beautiful, still morning. Malkit's father, his head bare and no shoes on his feet, swore at his wife and demanded an explanation. Naseebo told him of the eunuch and all that he had told her. Then, with rage burning in her eyes, she showed him the towel.

'LOOK AT IT!' she spat in disgust. 'You who brought this witch to our door...'

Malkit's father trembled as he took the white towel. An inferno began to blaze in his heart. He turned to Jagpreet.

'WHAT IS THIS?' he demanded.

Jagpreet, bewildered and afraid, found no words.

Her amber eyes filled with water as she began to shake.

'WHAT IS THIS?' he asked again. 'Has your father taken my *izzat,* you dirty whore . . . ?'

'I've done nothing wrong!' cried Jagpreet. 'PLEASE . . . !'

Malkit's father dropped the towel and took hold of Jagpreet's hair. He pulled her towards him, dragging her through the dirt. Malkit attempted to intervene, torn already between his love for Jagpreet and his family's honour. But his father pushed him aside and pulled Jagpreet up by her hair, punching and kicking at her.

'Drag this whore through the streets!' he proclaimed. 'Let everyone see what she is.'

'NO! NO!' Jagpreet screamed, but no one listened to her protests. No one came to help her as she struggled in vain to escape the clutches of her father-in-law.

Malkit's brothers tied Jagpreet's hands with thick rope. As she wept and wailed, Malkit could not bear to watch. Part of him longed to help his bride but he could not turn against his father. He winced as his sisters struck Jagpreet with stones and sticks. Unable to take any more he fled to his room, never turning back to his wife.

As she protested her innocence over and over, Jagpreet was kicked out into the village. For hours on end, she was pulled and pushed through the narrow lanes: spat at, kicked, punched and pummelled. Finally, when the fingers of dusk crept slowly across the sky, she lay discarded in a cornfield, left for dead.

Malkit locked himself in his room, crying and ashamed that he hadn't protected his bride from his family. But she had lied to them. Virgin brides bled on their wedding night, yet this girl had not. How could that be? The eunuch must have told his mother the truth. Yet the truth meant nothing as he sat in the dark. He thought of nothing except Jagpreet but couldn't find the courage to go to her. Family honour was far too important. Malkit, said my aunt, would regret his actions until his death some years later; a shattered and twisted shell of a man who never remarried.

I looked at my aunt, trying to hold back tears of my own and shaking my head. I didn't know what to say. What *were* you supposed to say? I couldn't believe that something so repellent had happened in my own family. I was disgusted.

'So did Jagpreet die in that field?' I asked my aunt, who was wiping away tears.

'No one knows, *beteh*. Her body was never found. Some people said that she was eaten by wolves, others that she was rescued by the eunuch and ended up as a prostitute. But a hermit woman, who lived out in those fields, told us that she had dragged herself to the nearby river and let herself fall in. No one knows the truth.'

'And the story about her going mad; where did that come from?' I asked.

'That was us,' replied my aunt, looking ashamed. 'We made it up to save her honour, even in death.'

'Oh...' I said, not knowing how else to respond.

'But Malkit's family told everyone that she hadn't been a virgin,' continued my aunt. 'His mother, Naseebo, carried the white towel with her for a while – as proof. It was a difficult time for our family and your grandfather could not handle the shame and the sadness. But it was all lies – I *knew* my sister and I *know* that she was a virgin on her wedding night. I *still* know it.'

'And that's why you reacted badly when you saw the blood on the towel after I'd cut my head?' I asked.

'Yes, *beteh*. That *one* towel, white, with crimson stains upon it, would have been enough to save my sister's life...'

Maisie sat perfectly still, her mouth open in shock, her pale blue eyes showing the horror she felt inside. I asked her if she was OK.

'Your aunt?' she asked in a whisper.

I nodded.

'But that's so horrible,' she added. 'I mean, how could they have killed her? Not all *women bleed when they have sex for the first time.'*

'That's what I thought when I heard the story,' I replied. 'Makes you think, doesn't it?'

This time Maisie nodded.

'All those times I talk about losing it and the jokes and stuff...' she said.

'For some British Asian girls losing your virginity isn't a joke.'

Maisie shook her head in disbelief.

'I think I wanna be sick,' she said.

FINDING IT

Anne Fine

FINDING IT

So now that break's over, I've got 10B for PSD. Or, as a normal person would say it, I'm taking over Miss Barker's Year 10 class for their lesson on Personal and Social Development.

That is school code for Sex and Drugs.

This week it's Sex. That's why I'm taking it. Miss Barker hasn't been teaching long enough to face down this unruly pack while she unfurls a condom over a banana. They'd tear the poor, shaking waif to shreds.

So they've got me instead. I've heard it all before – a million times. 'Please, Mrs Abbott, is it true that you can't catch a baby if you do it standing up?' 'Please, Mrs Abbott, Dai Wei says you don't get pregnant if it's your first time. He's lying, isn't he?' 'Please, Mrs Abbott . . . '

All teases, trying to get a rise out of me or a laugh from their mates. This lot must have had lessons on sex and drugs pretty well once a term since they were back in nursery. They're not like we were when we were their age, half of us ignorant enough truly to believe that it was safe if you did it up against a wall, or for the very first time.

This gang, they know it all. If they're not in the mood, they just complain. 'Oh, not *again*!'

'Miss! Miss! Can I do the banana trick? Pleeeeease!'

'Not fair! Surina did it last time, Miss!'

'Broke it in half!'

'Ouch!'

'Not letting her anywhere near *my* d—'

Here's where I step in. 'Finish that word out loud in this class, Rupert Henderson, and you are on report!'

They quieten down, and off we go. I give the same old lecture on differing levels of maturity, waiting until you feel ready, not giving in to peer pressure, and not believing everything you hear about what others are doing.

I illustrate it with a choice example from their own year-group. 'Remember when Tariq went round and asked you all if you were bothering to revise for exams?'

Tariq's expression sours. He won't forget they all said no, and most of them were lying.

'Well, it's like that,' I say. 'But it's far worse. Boys will tell girls that all the other girls are doing it because they think it'll improve their chances.'

I can hear Honor muttering, 'Well, some of us *are*,' but I pretend I can't, just to get on. 'As for you boys, can you imagine how unlikely it is that any one of you would ever be willing to stand up and admit you've never done it?'

Instantly Miguel-Angel is on his feet, of course. 'I've never done it.'

He takes a bow while they all jeer, 'Well, you're a *Catholic*!' as if that meant the poor boy didn't have the same equipment in his pants as they all do.

'Now, now,' I say. 'There's more than one good reason to remain a virgin.' And I can't help but think back to a time when there was only one.

Terror.

The terror of your mum and dad finding you out. The terror of catching something in those far off days when, if you saw your doctor, the surgery nurse was on the phone to tell your parents straight away. The terror of getting pregnant and having to leave school in shame. This lot don't know they're born. Our last head of history used to swear that that's the reason girls now outstrip the boys in almost every exam. 'Girls always put more into schoolwork,' he declared. 'But in the old days, by the time they reached the fifth form, a good half of the poor lambs were wasting the last two weeks of every month peering into their knickers, worrying themselves sick. Now contraception actually works, even our most committed turtledoves can finally concentrate.'

There's an improvement, then. But I still think they might be missing something. All that excitement. Even looking at a boy was pretty special back then. The lads stormed out of school, then sat perched on the railings at the bus station to hoot and crow as we girls filtered past in dribs and drabs into the bus bays. We all pretended we were deaf to teasing comments about how we looked, how short our skirts were, how we'd done our hair. We treated them as if they were invisible, or beneath contempt.

Things are so different now that so many of them are picked up in cars. No time to flirt if Mum's already craning out of something double parked, shrieking, 'Over here, Martin!' Where is the hinterland between the safety of the classroom and that more dangerous playground outside? There isn't one, so they all carry on just as they have since they were back in nursery, both sexes mucking about together all day long as if this school was one big communal playpen. Sometimes I come into the room on winter mornings to find that half the girls are lolling in their seats with their feet stuck up the boys' jumpers just for the warmth of it. And as often as not, the boys are simply leaning over those gorgeous, gaily-patterned legs to get on with the homework they should have done the night before.

Most of the boys I knew back then would—

Never mind all that! Back to the subject in hand.

'So,' I ask, 'what are the other reasons that we might have for choosing not to have sex?'

'Not wanting to be stoned to death,' Khatira mutters.

We all fall silent. Khatira's generally a quiet soul, so none of us is sure whether this is her idea of a bitter joke, or something horrible her family knows about from home.

It's Richard who rescues us. 'Because it's illegal and you might end up on one of those government pervo lists for life.'

I nod at him. 'Good one not to forget.'

'I've got a reason,' Bella shrieks. 'Because it might *hurt*.'

Quite why she gets a laugh, I can't imagine. She's raised a valid point. First time can really hurt. Fine if you're well anaesthetised with drink – and I expect that many of the faces grinning up at me may well be half-cut when they get it off for the first time. But parents used to be a good deal more parsimonious with pocket money than they are now, and even a bottle of the nastiest wine used to cost a small fortune. So most of us were pretty well stone cold sober while we were losing our virginity.

Why did we *do* it, then? I look back, and for the life of me I can't explain why, when I finally got away to university, it was with that pale streak Peter Parks that I actually reached what in my school days we had quaintly called 'Base 10'. I wasn't crazy about the boy. I wasn't even sure I really fancied him. I know my father had annoyed me mightily, claiming that he had to be gay simply because he wore pink shirts. ('Poofter' was actually the word Dad used. The days were yet to come when gays decided to rename themselves, and people like my parents would go round boring everybody rigid complaining that a perfectly good word that used to belong to everyone had suddenly been hijacked 'just for that lot'.)

Could it have been resentment that set me off? Oh, surely not! I can't believe I let my first time happen just to get back at my dad! (Not that he even knew. I would have died rather than let on I was doing it with anybody, even a crown prince with unassailably masculine credentials and no pink shirts at all.) And as it happens, Dad was right. Twenty years later I did catch sight of Peter on some late-night discussion show, talking about how he had finally realised his 'orientation'. (Another stolen word my dad would say. When I was young, it just meant working out exactly where you were on the map on the hike during the Sixth-Form Outdoor Day.)

But Peter didn't know that he was gay back then at university. He wanted sex, assumed he wanted it with me, and just kept on and on, begging and pleading. On and on and on. Not quite at the level of this lot when they want to work in pairs, or have a few more days to finish a project. 'Oh, please! Why *not*? Oh, go on, Mrs Abbott! Please!' But not far off. It's possible I found all Peter's pleading for sex so tiresome and repetitive I thought, if we just got it over with, we might be able to move on and talk about something else.

I certainly remember I wasn't prepared. None of those lubricants and unguents and gels you now see so shamelessly lying about were on the supermarket shelves back then to offer a clue to even the least observant shopper that losing it might not be plain sailing. All Peter and I had was the wobbly hook and eye fastening on the door to my rented attic room, a bit of hoping for the best, and several good hard shoves.

I can remember jack-knifing up with a bloodcurdling howl. 'Yeee-ow! That bloody *hurt*!'

Even my deaf old landlady mentioned the grim event at breakfast next morning. 'Did you hear cats in the night, dear?'

Convinced she realised that far cry was mine, I stared down at my plate. I was so miserable and so embarrassed. When Peter sat beside me in the lecture hall, I gathered up my notes and moved away. We didn't speak again till we were paired together at the end of the following week for a laboratory experiment in an exam. It wouldn't have looked good to ask to swap, so we just made the best of it – even went off for coffee afterwards in order to assure ourselves we'd understood the task and done things properly, and in the right order. And when we parted at the bus stop over an hour later, I reckon both of us were still pretending that the night we'd gone to bed together was just a mutual bad dream.

Not like these days. Sometimes, at break or lunchtime, I've sneaked into the music room to get a bit of extra marking done, and heard a couple of voices I know only too well from the back row in this class negotiating merrily under the window outside.

'Wanna come round to my gran's with me after school?'

'Sure she'll be out?'

'Line-dancing. Won't be back till six.'

'None of that stuff you tried on last week, though?'

'No. Sorry about that. Just saw a clip of it and thought, "That looks good fun. Ought to give that a try".'

'Well, sodding think again, Jamie, because it damn well *hurt*.'

'Yeah, well. Sorry, and all that.'

(Pause.)

'Well, *are* you coming or not?'

'S'pose I don't mind if I do.'

I can't believe they're going off to play with Jamie's grandma's Lego. But isn't it nice that they can tell each other what they want and what they like? I expect they're brilliant in bed, even at this age. We were so *clumsy*. I know I didn't get much chance to practise with Peter. (And maybe, bearing in mind the choice he made a few years down the line, he wouldn't have been quite the best partner for learning how to do it anyway.) But I just have this memory of trying to please one man after another, and never getting any satisfaction for myself, except the feeling I had done a good job.

On them. Not me.

Fat chance of any of the little ladies sitting in front of me now acting in such a self-sacrificial way. And good for them. It's nice to think that all these bananas haven't been thrown into the bin in vain. (The only member of staff who ever fancied them after they'd served their useful social purpose was Mr Browning; and ever since his doctor warned him that his potassium level had shot sky high, even he's started looking at them wistfully, and passing on by.)

Mind you, teaching this gang of know-it-alls how to put a condom on a banana is *ridiculous*. Sheer farce. Sometimes they're kind, and try to keep their faces straight. More often they are falling off their chairs with laughter. Who can blame them? You can bet your life that if we had a pulling-condoms-on-bananas competition, I'd still be fumbling to rip open the packet while they were busy setting up a one-day, inter-class, one-handed combat league, using their fully protected, ribbed, potassium-rich fruit swords.

But all this stuff's in the curriculum, so I ignore their rolling eyes and half-stifled sniggers, and carry on.

'Now you be careful, all of you,' I warn, 'to check that every packet that you use hasn't been tampered with.'

That sets them off again.

'Yes, Mrs Abbott. In case some weirdo's made a hole in it with a pin.'

'Or tipped chilli powder inside it.'

'Or sucked all the strawberry flavouring off already.'

'Shall we try being a bit more sensible, 10B?' I say, distracted. But finally, I get the damn thing out, and, placing it on top of the banana like the sort of fedora hat American gangsters wore in old films, I start to roll it down.

The whispering starts.

'She's handy at this job, isn't she?'

'That's years of practice, that is.'

'Of having sex with bananas!'

More peals of laughter run around the room. I raise my eyes to shoot a beady look at one or two of them, and suddenly can't help but imagine Georgina and Jamie on his grandmother's sofa, rolling and licking and groaning and thrusting, till they fall apart with a grin. There's nothing I can teach this lot. Their teenage competence is worlds away from my experience. It must have been years after knowing Peter that I even realised what sex was truly all about.

Could they *imagine* all those wasted years? Probably not. They'd have to understand that no one explained, and magazines weren't helpful, describing things in such a delicate way that, frankly, unless you already knew exactly what they were trying to tell you, you wouldn't grasp the point. There certainly weren't the pages of bluntly worded advice that you get now to help the tardy on the way to personal satisfaction. I swear that, until I was twenty-five I would have passed exams in differential calculus more easily than I'd have given myself a thrill.

Then I met Geoffrey.

'Don't touch! Don't touch me! I'm too ticklish. Stop it! Get off!' (And this was him, not me.) It took me weeks to chart which bits of him I could get near without him springing out of bed to clutch his pants over his private parts. 'You *promised* me! You said you wouldn't go anywhere near there! Look what you've done. You've set me off. Now I've got goose bumps!'

I defy anyone not to find someone like Geoffrey a challenge. He made a joke of it, of course. One night he came to bed wearing a mackintosh and welly boots. 'It's to protect myself. I need some sleep.' I cannot count the number of times one or the other of us fell out of bed, laughing our heads off.

'What are you *doing* up there?' demanded the girl from Uganda who rented the flat beneath.

'We're having sex,' said Geoffrey.

'It doesn't sound like any sex I know,' Masani countered irritably.

'That's because we're doing it wrong,' admitted Geoffrey. 'But one day we'll be bound to get it perfect, if only by accident, and after that I promise you we'll be more quiet.'

He was dead right. One day we got it perfect. I felt a shudder start. It wouldn't stop, and sheets of colour swept behind my eyes, over and over. Just sheets of colour falling – crimson and red and purple. There were explosions in my brain. I heard a far cry that I failed to recognise as my own voice till Geoffrey's hand came down over my mouth. 'Shhh! Shhh! We promised Masani we'd do it quietly once we got it right.'

Then we were laughing again.

An hour or so afterwards, I suggested we try again just to be sure we had the hang of it.

Geoff looked a little uneasy. 'You wouldn't rather get up and dressed, and do a nice jigsaw?'

'No. No, I wouldn't.'

So we did it again. And we've been doing it ever since, for more than twice as many years as any of 10B have been on the planet.

And that gives me another idea to try to set them thinking.

'What I'd like everyone to do now is sit and think about the number of times they've fallen in love, or had a crush, or really fancied someone. And I want you to think about how long each of those passions lasted and see how they average out.'

We have to take a bit of time out then, to revise how to do averages. But finally they are all set. I give them a bit of time to make the calculation, and then I say, 'Anyone willing to tell the rest how long they think they were in love each time?'

'Four days,' says Rupert.

'About a month,' says Lucy, copping an evil look from Jamie, whom I can only presume to be one of her many victims, and subject to a somewhat longer-lasting passion in his own right.

'Two years,' says Arif.

John Hestor turns to Honor. 'I was in love with you for one whole morning,' he says. 'But then I saw you eating a tuna sandwich with your mouth open, and went right off you.'

'Pillock!' snarls Honor.

'My mum has been in love with Elvis all her life,'

Surina says hastily, trying to spare her good friend Honor's blushes.

'The dead don't count,' I said. 'I only want you to think about the people you might have done it with, only to regret it soon after.'

When all the votes are in, and all abstentions counted, we reckon that the average passion that assails the members of 10B lasts eight weeks and three days.

'Not for me,' declares Miguel-Angel. 'When I finally fall in love, I'll be in love for *ever*. For *eternity*.'

And suddenly I think, 'Suppose he is?' and since I teach further maths as well as biology I can't help smiling because, if Miguel-Angel loves for infinity, then he will bring all of our averages up to infinity too. That's how infinity works.

It's a nice thought.

But I'm not going to tell them that, of course. Because the whole point of Sex and Drugs – sorry, Personal and Social Development – is to put 10B off. We do not want them having sex. We do not want them doing drugs. We want them here in class, as undistracted and as mentally alert as they can be.

We want them to pass their exams. Then they can all swan off and lose it any way they like with anyone they choose. I always say, so long as you have half a dozen GCSEs under your belt, you're a made man (or woman).

Then the buzzer sounds. Thank God. I peel the condom back off the banana and drop it into Miss Barker's PSD file, out of sight.

I hold up the banana. 'Anyone fancy this?'

'Wouldn't say no,' says Rupert. 'I forgot my lunch.'

I toss it to him.

'Right then,' I bellow over the rising din. 'Let me through first, if you don't mind.'

And I am out of there. Halfway along the corridor I peer through the glass in my own classroom door and catch Miss Barker's eye. She's sitting at my desk, trying to corral into a neater pile the blizzard of papers that's being thrust at her.

I wait until my usual class has disgorged into the corridor, then I go in.

'How were they?' I ask.

'Not bad at all,' she says. 'In fact, they mostly all sat quietly and just got on with it.'

She sounds surprised. Then she remembers her manners. 'What about my class?'

'Not bad at all,' I tell her. 'The banana played its part nicely enough. And Miguel-Angel claims that when he finally falls in love, it's going to be for ever.'

She laughs. But I can't help thinking of me and Geoffrey. So I hope Miguel-Angel's right. Because, if you want my opinion, losing it couldn't be less important. I am serious.

It's *finding* it that matters. That's what counts.

ABOUT THE AUTHORS

I had my first book for teenagers, *Creepers*, published when I was twenty-four and it was shortlisted for the Guardian Fiction Award. Since then I've written books for different age groups, but writing for that weird bit of life in between being a kid and being an adult is what interests me most. My other books for teenagers include *Warehouse*, *Malarkey* and *Ostrich Boys*, which was shortlisted for just about everything going, but eventually won the Royal Mail Scottish Book Award. When Andersen Press asked me to edit this anthology I jumped at the chance. It felt like an interesting, daring, important subject to explore. And I also got to choose my favourite authors to write for the collection.

I knew I was going to be a lifelong fan of **Jenny Valentine** from only three or four pages into *Finding Violet Park*, her Guardian-Award-winning debut novel. Her writing is as witty as it is wise, and displays a genuine empathy for her readers. Her subsequent books *Broken Soup* and *The Ant Colony* have sealed her reputation as a storyteller of the highest calibre, as well as earning shortlistings for several prizes, including the Booktrust Teenage Prize and Costa Children's Book Award. I was desperate to twist her arm to get her to contribute to *Losing It*. Luckily she said yes.

It would probably be impossible to consider putting together an anthology like *Losing It* without inviting **Melvin Burgess** to join in. He's one of the best-known, most successful and most daring writers we have for young people in the UK today. Famous for pushing boundaries and breaking taboos with novels such as the Carnegie-Medal-winning *Junk* and the Booktrust-Teenage-Prize-shortlisted *Doing It*, but he should perhaps also be regarded as a great experimenter with books like *Bloodtide* and *Sara's Face*. Whatever he's writing, you can be guaranteed it's going to make you think.

Patrick Ness had already garnered great critical acclaim for his adult fiction, but it was his first novel for teenagers *The Knife Of Never Letting Go* that brought him to a much wider audience. His 'Chaos Walking' trilogy has so far won him the Guardian Children's Fiction Prize, the Booktrust Teenage Prize and the Costa Children's Book Award – not to mention thousands and thousands of readers. He's an original and exciting writer, right at the forefront of all that's brilliant about writing for young people today.

Mary Hooper's reputation grows and grows with every new book. I loved her contemporary and insightful 'Megan' series of novels about a struggling young mum, but her *Newes From The Dead*, set in the seventeenth century, blew me away. It's a stunning evocation of time and place and character, and has won fantastic critical acclaim. I always knew when asking Mary to contribute to *Losing It* she'd produce a sensitive and perceptive story, no matter which period of history she chose to write about.

Girl, Missing shot **Sophie McKenzie** to fame when it won The Richard and Judy Best Kids' Book prize, and Sophie has been steadily gathering a loyal following of fans ever since, with *Blood Ties* – winner of the Red House Children's Book Award – and the 'Luke and Eve' and 'Medusa' series. Sophie's talent is to meld page-turning plots and sympathetic characters into cracking stories. I think that's why her fanbase has grown and grown, and why she often sweeps the board in book prizes where the readers themselves get to choose the winner.

Bali Rai is a unique voice in teenage fiction. He can move easily between hard-hitting, ultra-modern novels such as *The Crew* and its sequel *The Whisper*, to the magical realism of the semi-historical *City of Ghosts*. *Rani and Sukh*, his clever twist on *Romeo and Juliet*, earned a Booktrust Teenage Prize shortlisting. He's an author who likes to take risks and writes passionately, sometimes angrily, about the subjects that matter to him – making them matter to the reader too.

Anne Fine was the first writer I ever met and I soon discovered she was as funny and sharp and warm as the books she writes. Whether it's her Carnegie-Medal-winning *Flour Babies* and *Goggle Eyes*, or the more provocative *Road of Bones* and *Tulip Touch*, she proves time and again that she's one of the most admirable, affecting and entertaining writers for young people there's ever been. She was also a fantastic Children's Laureate from 2001 to 2003. I was delighted when she agreed to contribute a story to *Losing It*.

Keith Gray

The Absolutely True Diary of a Part-time INDIAN

SHERMAN ALEXIE

WINNER OF THE NATIONAL BOOK AWARD

'Son,' Mr P said, 'you're going to find more and more hope the farther and farther you walk away from this sad, sad, sad reservation.'

So Junior, who is already beaten up regularly for being a skinny kid in glasses, goes to the rich white school miles away. Now he's a target there as well. How he survives all this is an absolute shining must-read, and a triumph of the human spirit.

'Excellent in every way, poignant and really funny and heartwarming and honest and wise and smart.'
NEIL GAIMAN

9781842708446 £5.99

OUT OF SHADOWS

Jason Wallace

'Sometimes a book takes you somewhere and keeps you there, and this is one of them. Honest, brave and devastating, Out of Shadows *is more than just memorable. It's impossible to look away.'*
Markus Zusak, author of *The Book Thief*

Zimbabwe, 1980s
The war is over, independence has been won and Robert Mugabe has come to power offering hope, land and freedom to black Africans. It is the end of the Old Way and the start of a promising new era.

For Robert Jacklin, it's all new: new continent, new country, new school. And very quickly he learns that for some of his classmates, the sound of guns is still loud, and their battles rage on . . . white boys who want their old country back, not this new black African government.

Boys like Ivan. Clever, cunning Ivan. For him, there is still one last battle to fight, and he's taking it right to the very top.

'Excellent' Independent on Sunday

9781849390484 £6.99